MW00986407

"After my wife and I read *Schizophrenia: A Blueprint for Recovery*, it was like a light came on for us."

– Father of young person formerly in psychosis

"Milt Greek's thoughtful, respectful model for engaging psychotic individuals in treatment is welcome in a field that, in the past, had little to offer therapists who want to help individuals with schizophrenia."

– Sandy Watt, M.Ed. Professional Clinical Counselor

"Milt is one of the most articulate and astute authorities on schizophrenia I have ever had the privilege to know or hear."

– Tom Walker, NAMI Ohio Board of Trustees member

"Milt's experience and presentations are critical for those who work with persons with thought disorders."

– Diane Pfaff, MSW, Athens-Hocking-Vinton 317 Mental Health Board

Schizophrenia
A Blueprint for Recovery

Milt Greek

2012 Revised Edition

Schizophrenia: A Blueprint for Recovery

2012 Revised Edition

By Milt Greek

Published by Milt Greek

PO Box 475, Athens, Ohio 45701

For more information about this book and to purchase additional copies, visit

www.schizophreniablueprint.com

The author thanks Paul Komarek for his assistance in preparing this work for publication.

Cover Art Copyright 2012 by Jonathan Story, used with permission. The author wishes to express his appreciation to Jonathan for agreeing to allow his art to be used for this handbook.

Important Disclaimer

This book is intended for general educational purposes only. It does not substitute for individual medical advice from your doctor. Please consult your doctor for advice on your individual situation.

TABLE OF CONTENTS

PREFACE

During my early years in college, my life became more and more difficult. As problems grew and my life worsened, I gained insights into my life and my problems, but these insights alone didn't get my life back on track. As crisis followed crisis, my parents sought medical help for me, which at first I cooperated with, but then grew hostile towards because the medical establishment kept locking me up in mental hospitals and ignoring my insights and issues.

By a series of coincidences and with the help of friends, I came to the surprising realization that I was suffering from schizophrenia, as the doctors had been saying, and needed to take medication to get control of my life. After I accepted my diagnosis, I stabilized on medication but fell into deep depression, sleeping fourteen hours a day for the next two years. Despite this problem, I managed to finish degrees in psychology and sociology.

Unable to find work with my degrees, I retrained in computer programming. In spite of ongoing depression, I left welfare and worked without insurance for five years, finally gaining enough experience to receive insurance through work and stabilize my life economically. I eventually returned to the town where I had gone to college and met the woman who is now my wife.

With my wife's help I began to review the issues and delusions that had made up my mental illness. At the same time, I volunteered to help a couple of people who were in the psychotic stage of the illness and formed a schizophrenia peer support group. During these years my depression ended and I gained insights into the nature of schizophrenia. The result of this process is a blueprint for recovery which is described in this guidebook. Beginning with an explanation of the formation of the delusional framework and suggestions for ways to work with actively psychotic people, the blueprint discusses steps to move people from post-delusion lethargy into self-understanding and reintegration into mainstream society. Despite the brevity of this guidebook, the blueprint describes a process that took over ten years of my life. This time frame may be shorter or longer depending on the individual.

The material in this book is meant to provide people with schizophrenia, family members, and mental health workers insight into means of transforming a situation of seeming hopelessness into one of renewed strength and vitality. Its value lies not in dogmatic interpretation, but in being applied as befits each individual case. Those aspects of this book which prove useful in some cases may be less useful in others. Paying close attention to what works for a particular individual is key to working with a psychotic individual. The extent to which this guidebook provides the basis for insight into individual cases is the degree to which it is successful. I sincerely hope that it may provide help and comfort to you and your particular situation.

Milt Greek

INTRODUCTION TO 2012 REVISED EDITION

Since the writing of this handbook in 2006 and 2007, I have wanted to add more material. Some of this additional material was included in the 2009 recordings on DVDs detailing this material in seven talks. While I had hoped to complete these additions in 2010, new volunteer work cropped up, limiting the time I had to devote to this revision. In 2011, I set time aside for presenting and/or attending at five conferences involving schizophrenia and recovery and undertook a pilot survey of ten people in post-psychosis. These activities gave me a more complete sense of the role of this material in the larger community and rounded out my own views of schizophrenia and recovery.

The revisions contained in this work are mainly enhancements in understanding psychosis and a discussion of medication and alternatives. The additional material on psychosis is mainly in Chapter One and Appendices B and C.

At present there is a hotly debated question of medication verses non-medication and strong feelings on all sides about its use or nonuse. Some caregivers are committed to using medication; other caregivers are committed to not using medication. The updates on medication are attempts to make the approach in this handbook useful for both groups.

The purpose of this handbook is to provide a set of components that can be used independently of each other. As such, I have written this handbook to allow for people to use what works for their specific situation and to ignore what is not effective. It is important to view each person and their surroundings as unique and to apply these components as best fits with that unique situation. To the extent this handbook provides a variety of means to do this, it is successful.

Milt Greek, 2012

CHAPTER ONE
THE BUILDING OF
SCHIZOPHRENIC PSYCHOSIS

This chapter explains how psychosis slowly builds, the experiences which give people with schizophrenia a strong belief in our delusions, and the underlying reality which people with schizophrenia perceive. This explanation will help the reader understand why we actively cling to delusions and what our behavior and attitudes are seeking to achieve. It will serve as a basis for the next chapter, which details approaches for working with the psychotic person and moving the person toward accepting diagnosis and a commitment to use medication.

Schizophrenic thinking has a number of basic elements that affect the forming of psychosis. Over time the elements gradually create a delusional framework that is usually fully in place when the person's problem comes to the attention of family and mental health workers. This delusional framework poses one of the toughest problems in working with psychotic people and persuading them to accept their diagnosis and take medication.

Chemical Imbalance Like Continuous LSD Trip

To understand how schizophrenia affects perception, it is important to start with the recognition that schizophrenia creates a situation where we experience hallucinations, voices, and other effects like a constant LSD trip. The experience is like unwittingly being given LSD every day for years on end. As a result, hallucinations and unusual thinking gradually become a constant part of everyday life. We have strange experiences, with increasing frequency and intensity, and we begin to develop ideas about the world around us and our own lives based on these experiences.

Basic rules of perception that we had known prior to schizophrenia are lost and in their place we develop new ways of thinking that mirror our new, hallucinatory reality. Arguing that we should return to the old rules of perception is a frequent and useless practice, since the new rules we apply match our daily experiences.

Loss of Object Permanency and the Flow of Realities

Object permanency is the psychological name for our belief that objects exist after they have disappeared from sight. It was described by the French child psychologist Jean Piaget, who noted that very young infants would forget about balls and other toys with which they were playing once the objects rolled out of sight. Piaget noted that after reaching a certain age, the children began to look for the missing toy, indicating they understood it still existed.

During psychosis, we lose object permanency. Hallucinations and other aspects of our experience indicate that objects actually do fade in and out of existence. Often, this can occur in a matter of moments. As a result, we come to believe that things and people appear and disappear for mystical reasons. For example, if I were going to a store and met a friend on the way, I would believe the chance appearance of my friend was closely connected to a higher purpose that was being fulfilled by my trip. In addition to whatever mundane purpose I had for going to the store, I might be attempting to change reality through a ritual involving money and purchases, and I would see my friend as someone whose presence indicated a central role in this ritual.

In place of object permanency, we develop the belief we are centered in a flow of multiple realities and potential futures that might be entered into at any moment. In normal life, choices such as in what community to live, what to do for work, for whom to work, and who to have as a spouse create long-term changes in one's destiny. For a person with schizophrenia, the possibility of entering into various futures is immediate and can be caused by any minor event or choice, such as to whom to talk or what magazine to read. This immediacy mirrors the hallucinatory experience, where minor events can trigger major hallucinatory episodes that seem to indicate a massive change in reality.

Since we have lost object permanency, we lose the concept of boundaries in time and place. Places, events and beings that are thought to exist outside of mundane reality—such as heaven, hell, the rapture, angels, gods and demons—can enter into this earthly reality and we can be taken into their reality at any time. Instead of the static physical reality the normal individual assumes, the person lives in a place where, in a matter of moments, small thoughts or actions can bring about eternal heaven on earth for everyone, or the end of the world and all creation being cast into the depths of hell. It is with this dramatic backdrop that people with schizophrenia view daily events.

Multiple Realities vs. Separation from Reality

Psychosis is commonly defined as being separated from reality, but is it much more accurate to view it as a consciousness which believes that there are multiple realities in addition to the commonly perceived consensus reality. The person's belief in multiple realities also perceives the additional realities as having more importance than the consensus reality. Much of our inability to deal with day to day reality comes from our need to act on the belief that these more significant realities take precedence over the reality we all perceive.

An example of this thinking would be that we may know that we are in a psychiatric hospital, but we may believe that we are simultaneously in an unearthly spiritual realm and some of the people and things in the hospital are actually from the spiritual realm and are on Earth with a special mission to transform us and others in some way. We will be focused on the spiritual transformation we believe is occurring and we will respond to events according to our view that this spiritual transformation is of paramount importance. Whether we believe that the spirits/people around us are benevolent or malevolent is dependent on other delusions and on how the hospital staff and patients appear to help or hinder our spiritual quest.

Group vs. Unique Experience Defining Reality

Central to our new perceptions of reality is a loss of the commonly held group definitions of reality and a replacement of this source of "truth" with a focus on unique individual experiences defining reality. In normal human culture, most people define reality through a loose collection of group beliefs that reflect one's personal world. For example, people in some parts of the United States may have consensus that the Bible is the source of truth about the spiritual world and world history, but may disagree on which books and chapters in the Bible are the most important in guiding our lives today. On the other hand, people elsewhere in the United States may believe that Darwin's theory of evolution and historical, archeological, and anthropological studies are the determiner of knowledge about these things and have consensus beliefs about the spiritual world (or lack of it) and world history stemming from these sources. Individuals within these two subcultures will generally define reality according to the group consensus around them and when members of one subculture come into contact with members of the other subculture there is often conflict and disbelief at how little the other knows about "truth."

Within hallucinatory perceptions, events that seem very real and of utmost universal importance—such as portents of the end of the world or revelations of potentially wonderful changes for the world—seem to be delivered to us in epiphanies. These events are often connected symbolically to our inner emotional nature and seem related to our real life histories. We believe we are being shown a mysterious and all-encompassing reality that underlies ordinary reality. We are well aware that if we hadn't had these unique experiences we would not believe as we do, yet we perceive these experiences as actual events of great importance.

In line with these experiences, we develop a very strong belief that individual revelation, rather than group consensus, is the key to uncovering true knowledge. As discussed in Appendix B on common delusions experienced by a small group of post-psychotic men, we often come to believe that the majority of people are in a state of numbness and ignorance, suffering from a sort of spiritual mind-control that blinds common people to the epiphanies that are so obvious to us. As a result, when we say things like we have met God or there are angels, demons, aliens, or similar entities presently on the Earth, we are basing these beliefs on perceptions of actual or hallucinatory events. When people respond that this is not possible, we almost invariably feel that "You weren't there, so how do you know?" While frustrating to the treatment team, this challenging attitude is actually a statement of a solid empirical axiom and should not be rejected out of hand. When people around us tell us that these things don't happen, even though they were not present when we witnessed them, it drives us into the company of those who do believe in such events and away from the treatment team. (Ways to handle this dilemma are discussed in Chapter Two.)

Synchronicity and Confusion

People with schizophrenia develop thinking based on synchronicity, a term coined by psychoanalyst Carl Jung to describe thoughts connecting to outside events. Prophetic dreams are an example of synchronicity.

People often observe synchronicity early in their illness and are intrigued by the spiritual and practical possibilities they pose. We believe that synchronicities indicate the possibility for the mind to magically affect the world, and often seek to do things that increase synchronicity in our lives. We begin to see connections—real or imagined—behind these events. The real events of synchronicity give strength to a mystical or religious view of the world that becomes the basis for our new way of thinking.

We begin to search the world for religious or symbolic structures underlying events in our world. These symbolic structures are like those theorized by Jung in his studies of symbols across cultures. Our search to uncover mystical knowledge is affected, however, by our inner turmoil. Our inner emotions are projected poetically onto the symbols we develop and make the symbolic system a deeply personal one, rather than one that applies to humanity and the universe. The underlying feelings indicated by the delusions can provide insight into the inner turmoil and issues hidden by the confused behavior and communication that are the hallmark of psychotic people. For example, people who are harming themselves or who believe that they are condemned by God are usually struggling with a moral dilemma in their real life.

We come to believe that the religious/symbolic system we think we are uncovering can ritually or magically be used to bring about miracles, either for ourselves or for the world as a whole. We attempt to manipulate these symbols through ritual or symbolic action, in hopes of finding a magical solution to our problems and the problems of the world. With the world-view that heaven or hell might occur at any time, we look for magical means to bring about heaven on earth. This search often results in odd behavior, including decorating our rooms and houses in unusual ways, small quirks of behavior, repeated phrases or expressions that seem meaningless to others, and sometimes more dramatic and occasionally dangerous attempts to ritually bring about a miraculously better world.

Accurate Intuitions during Hallucinations and Psychosis

One of the most validating aspects of psychosis for people experiencing it is the common phenomenon of accurate intuitions during psychosis, including as part of a hallucinatory episode. These accurate intuitions often provide insight and even guidance to the person, making us believe fervently that the experiences of psychosis are all meaningful. Accurate intuitions give us the belief that we are becoming aware of an underlying spiritual world that unites all life and uncovering this spiritual world becomes part of our personal goals during psychosis.

A recent survey I undertook of ten post-psychotic people asked individuals about their experiences with events that supported their belief in their delusions, including accurate intuitions. At the time of this writing the surveys are still being reviewed by objective evaluators, but by my estimation at least four of the ten people reported instances of accurate intuitions during psychosis. In one case, a woman reported being on horseback and seeing a man in long flowing robes riding a horse. From this the woman sensed that she should return home and soon afterwards a storm blew up. Since riding during a storm could have been dangerous, the woman regarded the event as helpful. In another case, a man reported repeated accurate intuitions, including predicting to his counselors that his wife would have a car accident. The wife did, in fact, have a car accident, but instead of acknowledging the validity of the man's experience the therapist reported the man to the police for possibly trying to harm his wife.

Accurate intuitions pose some of the more difficult phenomenon to explain with the mindset of many normal counselors. It is crucial to understand that the events are actually common during psychosis. Attempting to argue that these experiences are not valid is not only counterproductive, it is a failure to understand the complexity of the psychotic experience and devalues the person who is experiencing it. In place of attempting to dismiss actual events with a close-minded approach to life experiences, it is more important to acknowledge the validity of the experiences and work to help the person distinguish between actual events and jumping to false conclusions based on these events. (Again, Chapter Two discusses means to achieve this.)

Visions of Probable Futures, Static, and Confusion

During psychosis, people experience hallucinations that vary from minor, such as how a person's eyes might appear, to major episodes, in which reality seems to be in flux. Some hallucinations have no unusual qualities, and seamlessly blend with ordinary reality. These hallucinations are only recognized as such after the person asks other people present during the hallucinations if they saw the same thing.

Hallucinations may seem nonsensical to outsiders, but some hallucinations are actually intuitive images of possible future realities. A minor example of that occurred during my psychosis when I was about to enter a room that I knew another guy was in, but heard his voice say, "Let me open the door." I stood outside the door and waited for a few moments, after which the guy opened the door and walked out. There were no windows in the door or room, so I had no visual clue that he was about to walk out the door.

A more powerful example of the visionary quality of some hallucinations is described in Appendix A on the series of hallucinations I had involving God, Jesus, heaven, and hell. Those hallucinations, along with others that I had during psychosis, exemplify the strong symbolic and intuitive aspects that make many hallucinations deeply and personally meaningful.

Mixed in with the symbolic and visionary hallucinations are hallucinations that amount to static. These can be random voices, sounds, and sometimes frightening experiences that seem to be indicating some impending or actual event. Because of the occasional accurate intuitions that we experience, we tend to believe all of our unusual experiences are real and meaningful. In these instances, we believe that we are being shown a deeper aspect of reality, and will have the accurate, intuitive experiences as proof that the hallucinations are meaningful and significant.

People with schizophrenia combine the discovery of synchronicity with the visions of probable futures in an attempt to ritually manifest the best reality that can be imagined. Through a combination of synchronicity, magic, religious experience, ad hoc rituals, symbolic actions, and other forms of magical action, people will pursue the best probable future that their hallucinations and delusions point them toward. In some cases, this involves fanciful dreams of being on the doorstep to a heavenly realm; in others, this involves desperate and sometimes self-destructive or violent attempts to stave off worldwide catastrophe.

Voices and Dialogues

Most people have a single voice in their mind that they identify as their own. During schizophrenia, the central voice in our mind breaks down and is replaced by a cacophony of various voices, similar to the experience people sometime have when they are drifting off to sleep and different voices seem to be having conversations independently of their own voice.

The central voice acts not only as a single source of thought, but also as a censor for any thoughts that we strongly dislike. When it breaks down, the various other voices often express distressing or horrible thoughts that we would never think on our own. For example, one schizophrenic friend who was stridently against racism had a racist voice in his mind. During his psychosis, one of his greatest concerns was this racist voice and the possibility that he himself was racist. This was despite the fact that he was friends with people of different races.

It is my supposition that the voices we experience have a basis in dialogues between ourselves, our family, and members of our community. We develop strong impressions of how those around us think and these viewpoints shape us unconsciously. Our central voice develops in response to these dialogues and our thoughts are, in fact, our reply to others around us. In social psychology, this view is summarized in the works of George Herbert Mead and his theory of the I/Me.

When our central voice breaks down, the impressions left by those close to us become autonomous voices, speaking independently and chaotically. The voices can be very loud within our own mind, or can sometimes be heard outside our head. Mixed in with these voices are hallucinations of accurate intuition, as mentioned above. Once the voices become autonomous, they develop seemingly superhuman nature, becoming the voices of angels, demons, gods, goddesses, and other spirits. They become very difficult to resist.

As is common within families and communities, people with schizophrenia often grow up in situations where there are a number of strong-willed people who disagree with each other. The impressions received by a normal person growing up usually contain contradiction and conflict about what view of reality is true and should be followed. In the same way, the voices that we experience in schizophrenia represent basic contradictions in the sentiments of the family and community around us. In the seeming form of superhuman voices, however, the contradictions in which people with schizophrenia grew up become another layer of dramatic and frightening landscape in which we are torn between contradictory voices alternately condemning and uplifting us.

For outside observers, getting information about the family and community in which the person grew up can illuminate connections between the voices heard in childhood and the voices experienced as supernatural in psychosis. Understanding the dramas of these real life contradictions and imagining them as being acted out in extremely exaggerated and overwhelming fashion in the supernatural voices can help give insight into the psychotic inner world.

Double Binds of Reality

People are usually caught in double binds in the real world around them. These double binds can be both personal and universal, often have a moral dimension, and also will often be part of the contradictions in views and values that exist in the families and communities around the person. In the case of the schizophrenic person with the racist voice, he had both racist and stridently anti-racist members in his family and community, and he felt torn by his privileges as a white person. His disease resulted in a racist voice and anxiety around people of other races, but he felt compelled to be friends with a diversity of people and struggled successfully to be friends with people of other races. As mentioned before, one of his greatest concerns was the resolution of the double bind between racism, anti-racism, and his privileges as a white person.

The double binds create conflicting pressures and demands. Solving these double binds often becomes an obsession, even though the contradictions are often too great to be resolved by a single person, healthy or otherwise. Unable to resolve these conflicts through mundane actions and experiencing hallucinations and delusions that express the emotional conflict symbolically, people with schizophrenia will seek to find magical solutions to real life problems. For example, people concerned about the real world ecological crisis will seek to find ways to control the weather and reverse global warming through magic. They will also come up with difficult and sometimes impractical solutions to problems, such as deciding not to drive or ride in cars, buses, or other vehicles that add to global warming.

Poetic Expression of Reality

The feelings of people with schizophrenia about reality are expressed poetically in both normal thoughts and hallucinations. This poetic expression of reality appears in the form of hallucinations seen as actual events which confirm the deepest feelings about reality.

Once these symbolic ideas appear to manifest as concrete reality, they take on a life of their own. Instead of treating the hallucinations as symbolic visions of deeply personal feelings, the person misinterprets hallucinations as actual reality with universal implications. The person then responds to events as if these symbolic events were real and attempts to solve the dilemmas they create with sometimes wild or extreme acts.

For example, during psychosis I had a hallucination described in Appendix A during which I met Jesus. The experience was a symbolic expression of real life choices I faced between pursuing positive or negative paths which had origins in both my family and my community and which had universal implications in today's world. I responded to this symbolic experience with believing that I had been condemned by God to hell and that the rapture was beginning in subtle but expanding ways. I then began to act very wildly, as a normal person would if the rapture really were unfolding before one's eyes.

Hallucinations and False Perceptions

As shown in the example above, the hallucinations create false perceptions that seem based in concrete reality. Many hallucinations blend seamlessly with reality or express symbolically the innermost reality of people with schizophrenia. As such, hallucinations connect on a tremendously personal and real level, and seem to confirm what people feel about themselves, their reality, and the challenges they and the world face. Since hallucinations are frequently the poetic and intuitive expression of real problems that people cannot express clearly or directly, they are often valued as experiences which confirm their identity in the midst of contradiction, double binds, and crises.

If the person with schizophrenia were to take the hallucinations as symbolic expressions of personal reality, as works of fiction meant to be pondered for their personal meaning, the process of recovery would be easier and help with the healing of the contradictions and double binds in and around the person. Hallucinations, however, appear to be real, and create false perceptions that compound the problems surrounding the person.

Hallucinations, voices, and other sources of confusion build a delusional framework over time. These experiences create a concrete basis for delusions and make symbolic events more real than the problems the symbols represent. As a result, real life problems become mixed chaotically with symbolic and delusional beliefs, submerging the original problems beneath the symbolic delusions the person develops about them.

Projection of Meaningful Symbols into Delusions

A central source of confusion for the person is that there is often projection of symbols of the person's deeply held feelings into their hallucinations and delusions. Since the experiences of the hallucinations appear to be real events, the person often takes the symbols literally and believes that the events have universal, rather than personal, implications. As such, personal symbolic events involving deities, angels, demons or aliens are taken are actual events and highly delusional beliefs arise from the experiences.

The delusional beliefs result from a misinterpretation of the events. The hallucinatory events that have meaning could be taken as metaphors for one's life and the world as a whole, to be decoded and understood within that framework. In the psychotic state, however, the literal interpretation of events leads the person to fully embrace symbolic messages as actual. In an example from Appendix A, where I recount a series of hallucinations involving God and Jesus, I mistook a symbolic experience as literal events, leading me to conclude that Jesus was back on Earth and the Rapture was slowly unfolding before my eyes. It is this grandiose generalization that marks the delusional framework and causes a tremendous amount of stress for the person experiencing psychosis.

Stepwise Building of a Delusional Framework

The experiences of a person with schizophrenia create a complex delusional framework built step by step over time. This framework is the result of the ongoing personal history in the months and years prior to diagnosis. The delusional framework will be supported by real life experience, real life double binds and problems, and accurate intuition. As a result, the person will strongly believe in this delusional framework.

By the time the person's behavior becomes clearly dysfunctional, the delusional framework is largely controlling the person's perceptions. People who enter into the person's life will be seen from the perspective of this framework. People with schizophrenia will develop delusions about the people they meet, assigning them a place in their dramatic and personal system of symbols. The framework will take on a life of its own, explaining events and confirming delusions through various concrete events.

Being an Emotional Sponge

People with mental illness absorb emotions from others. Emotional reactions in people with schizophrenia will often be stronger than in the person who originally had the feeling. For example, a person with schizophrenia might be exposed to someone who is angry about politics. After a certain length of time around the angry person, the person with schizophrenia will become very upset. However, since the emotion is interpreted through a delusional framework, the person may become angry at things seemingly unrelated to the discussion, or turn the anger inward with self-destructive acts, or act out a symbolic ritual to magically solve a delusional problem that the upsetting emotion evokes.

Negative emotions that the person absorbs are frequently turned into symbolic problems that don't seem related to the original source. The person will then attempt to solve the symbolic problem through magical rituals. In some cases, these acts will go unnoticed by others, such as when I responded to tension in my family home by secretly turning certain books in our bookcase upside down in what I thought was a magical reversing of negative energy. In other cases, exposure to negative emotions will result in the person acting out wildly and sometimes dangerously.

Magical Quest of Fully Developed Psychosis

When I surveyed a group of ten post-psychotic individuals, seven of the ten clearly indicated a belief that they were on a magical or spiritual quest during psychosis. One person's answer was not clear. The remaining two people who described their psychosis either described a short-term incident or experienced full psychosis only briefly before realizing that they were hallucinating/delusional. From these results, I believe that the perception that we are on a spiritual or magical quest is a very common aspect of fully developed psychosis.

The belief in the spiritual quest is created by the evolution of the delusional framework, interweaving real life events, metaphorical visions, accurate intuitions, and other things that create a new view of the world in which reality can be miraculously changed for the better through mind over matter. We become preoccupied with this possibility, seeing it as a dramatic and reliable way to resolve both our problems and the world's problems through our newly discovered insights and abilities.

Attempts to directly thwart this magical quest are met with suspicion and disregard. We have many events supporting our beliefs and perceive the attempt to stop us as sign that the person is either a person who is mind-controlled and ignorant of the true nature of the world or, worse yet, part of an evil conspiracy to bring about a horrible calamity on the Earth.

Knowing that the magical quest is a central part of psychosis allows outsiders to apply a formula to help understand the beliefs and motivations of the person in psychosis. This formula is not meant to serve as a means to contradict the beliefs, but rather to aid others in sincerely allying themselves with the good seeds that are at the root of this quest. Such alliances help calm the person in psychosis and allow, in the long run, the transition of the magical quest for worldwide transformation into a personal spiritual journey which seeks to bring about the same better world, but this time through less grandiose and more practical means.

The formula for understanding the beliefs and intentions of the person in psychosis is:

Person's background + Person's issues of concern + Projection of background and issues in symbolic form + Magical thinking = Beliefs and direction of magical quest.

Real life examples of this analysis include:

— A person concerned about global warming who has magical thinking attempts to split clouds with his mind as the first step to learning how to magically reverse global warming.

— A person from a liberal white family with racist people in both their extended family and community and suffers from the projection of these racist voices in the form of uncontrolled and unwelcomed racist statements entering his thoughts expresses deep concerns about needing to control these racist voices, including through ritual and other magical means.

— A person who has an accurate intuition of a friend's death from low blood sugar, causing an anxiety attack that is marked by the idea that he, too, has dangerously low blood sugar amounts followed a series of delusions and hallucinations about his own death.

— A person with a scientific mindset who has concerns about ecology evolves an end of the world scenario that includes good aliens active on Earth and trying to help humanity while evil aliens seek to do harm.

— A person who has intergenerational patterns of sexist abuse in the family and adopts spiritual mysticism during psychosis develops a sanctifying of feminine principles and a quest to uncover "the divine secrets of feminine."

It should be noted that having insight into the spiritual quest of the person not only creates an understanding of the mindset of the person in psychosis, but also clues about ways to bring about healing resolutions to the inner turmoil and stress that fuels the perceptions of an impending crisis. Drawing from with doctoral thesis of Paris Williams, it is possible to identify different types of psychotic content and different locations of the psychotic delusions. For example, in one of the journeys through psychosis that Dr. Williams discusses, a man called Byron has deeply visionary experiences during psychosis, seeking to explore spiritual realms and bring knowledge back to humanity. In these experiences, the man saw images and had experiences that in later years he was able to recognize within the teachings of Tibetan Buddhism. Following a Tibetan Buddhist Lama as a teacher allowed Byron to attain a healing resolution for his experiences, giving them meaning and context within that tradition.

In a different example, a woman called Cheryl experienced extreme self-loathing during her psychosis, plagued by voices that expressed deep-seated and exaggerated feelings of rejection and worthlessness, especially as a partner and family member. Working through these deeply held feelings by coming to resolve within herself that she is lovable and worthy—despite ongoing internal emotional patterns otherwise—and eventually connecting with the love of her family and a partner resolved the inner turmoil that overwhelmed her during psychosis.

During psychosis, the inner emotional turmoil creates an ongoing sense of trouble that must be relieved by solving real problems through symbolic acts. People with schizophrenia will usually be on a quest to solve the various problems in their lives and the world around them when concerned family members, friends, and mental health workers encounter them. As people attempt to help them by chemical therapy, individuals with schizophrenia will be determining if these people appear helpful to their quest to magically solve real life and symbolic problems. The combination of these two directions will create the events that follow the initial diagnosis of schizophrenia.

Chapter Two
Working with Someone in Psychosis

At the present time, working with a person in psychosis is usually seen as a situation where reason and dialogue are useless. The primary means of treating psychotic individuals are a collective insistence on taking medication, by force if necessary, repeated and forced hospitalizations, and similar tactics that amount to wrestling people with schizophrenia to the ground and holding them under lock and key until they surrender to the will of the medical establishment. One of the problems with this approach is that by treating the psychotic aspects of the schizophrenia, it inflames the paranoid aspects and can frequently worsen symptoms before improving them.

Recognizing how a person thinks as described in the previous chapter is a means of establishing a positive dialogue with the rational core of the individual and moving him or her to a place of consenting with the medical treatment. This process has numerous components and is explained in the "mentor" section later in this chapter. This process should occur simultaneously with efforts by others who are seeking to get the person to take medication, referred to in this chapter as the "realists."

Creating a Positive Environment - Family and Friends

There are a number of things that family and friends can do to help a person with schizophrenia. One of the simplest and most effective is to create a positive environment around the person. Since people with schizophrenia are emotional sponges, they absorb negativity and are very adversely affected by harsh emotions. When family and friends eliminate sources of negativity, such as newscasts, media violence, and similar things, they will find that the person will be calmer, easier to deal with, and more willing to compromise with others. The person's delusions will also be more positive and less pressing, since the emotions of the people around him or her indicate that things are okay.

To avoid negativity, it is important to be aware of how television and other media affect mood and paranoia. The highly energetic and quick-flowing events of television can be very confusing to people with schizophrenia and can aggravate symptoms by being a source of hallucination and delusion. Television is also filled with negativity that may not seriously affect sane people, but which can severely disturb a person with schizophrenia. It is not unusual for people with schizophrenia to believe that events on television are in some way real and pertinent to their lives, even though the programming may be completely fictional.

It is also important to remember that sources of comedy should not be too dark and to clearly separate satire from reality, since people with schizophrenia think in very literal and naïve ways, and therefore have a hard time separating sarcasm and double meanings from actual meanings. It is not unusual for people with schizophrenia to take sarcastic or ironic statements as statements made in complete seriousness.

Talking about happy subjects around the person with schizophrenia is a positive way to improve his or her mood. Happy memories, good times with family and friends, enjoyable hobbies, and other sources of happiness make for good topics of conversation. For family to remember happier times and good events around them is also helpful to the family members during the hard times of psychosis. If a person with schizophrenia walks in on a serious talk, change the subject when the chance arises. Avoid discussing violence, news, world problems, politics, religion and other subjects that can evoke negative feelings unless the talk involves positive aspects, such as good news about the world. Even so, discussing things that create powerful emotional responses is usually not a good idea since people with schizophrenia tend to have such strong emotions.

If the person with schizophrenia brings up a difficult subject, be honest with the person and treat him or her compassionately. Listen to the person's concerns and make note of them, since they often provide clues to the inner experience of the individual. While it is natural to want to provide reassurance, often the person's discussion of hard topics will be motivated by deeply held beliefs and powerful experiences, and one should observe if the reassurance is accepted by the individual. It is important not to gloss over difficult subjects people with schizophrenia are concerned about, such as ecology, war, violence, bigotry and other social, community, or family problems. Glossing over these subjects alienates people and convinces them that the person is trying to dissuade them from finding a solution to these problems, and therefore is part of the group that is causing the problem.

A way to improve the mood is to focus on beauty, especially natural beauty. Taking walks in natural areas, enjoying a beautiful day, finding pictures of rainbows, waterfalls, beautiful landscapes, and other sources of beauty can be very helpful to a person's mood. If it is at all possible, taking regular family walks in natural areas or in the surrounding neighborhood can provide both the exercise and the relaxation that will help people deal with their sense of crisis and impending disaster, serving to ease tension created by worry.

As difficult as it may be when someone you care about is experiencing psychosis, having a sense of humor is an important way of relieving the stress that everyone feels. Trying to be light-hearted and optimistic between difficulties can send signals to the person that all is well.

The diet of a person with schizophrenia should be balanced and have a lot of Vitamin B-complex in it. Ideally, it should include dark green vegetables, leafy greens (excluding iceberg lettuce), wheat germ if possible, and fruit and citrus juices. This will help boost the person's neurological system and will provide a healthy feeling to the body.

Providing the person with a sense of belonging and being loved is also a very direct way to help calm the person. Family members and close friends can help the person by touching, hugging, and showing affection in action and speech. Telling the person that you love him or her and that he or she is important to you is a way to ease paranoia and build a sense of safety. It is important, however, to be aware of how the person reacts to being touched. Due to personal history and a number of other factors, the person may enjoy being touched by one person but may find being touched by someone else stressful. Trial and error will distinguish the two.

Another means to encourage a calm and positive mood is to have the individual listen to positive and beautiful music and see positive art. People with schizophrenia are often artistic and have an appreciation of beauty, so exposing them to art that is beautiful and music that is soothing is helpful. In some cases, people with schizophrenia may enjoy being read to from books, including children's books such as Winnie-the-Pooh.

Encouraging people with schizophrenia to express themselves artistically is also helpful. Playing music, drawing, painting, sculpting of clay or wood are all ways that people can express their inner emotions and feelings. Encouraging artistic expression and other habits that people enjoy can help move them toward a calmer, happier, and more receptive mood.

Connecting with the Schizophrenic Person - Family, Friends, and Counselors

In working with a person with schizophrenia, it is important to make up for the lack of clear communication by paying attention to body language and other means of communicating. Watch for underlying emotions and moods. Pay attention to the person's eyes, mouth, face, and body language to get a sense of how the person is feeling.

Note changes in mood as people, topics of conversations, and events occur and discuss possible connections with friends and family.

Be aware of when the person with schizophrenia is showing feelings that don't match what is being said, such as when the individual seems happy about an unhappy topic. This is an indicator of an inner contradiction and can be a sign of either a double bind or of a situation of conflict in the person's family or community that has become a center of conflict within the person.

Also be aware of when the person with schizophrenia seems to be carrying weight or is reacting to being demeaned. To keep communication open with the person, it is important to convey respect despite the difficulties in communication and behavior. There is a tendency, for example, for people to talk about people as if they were not there. This tendency needs to be counteracted and respect needs to be shown to the person. In one instance, I had just met with a deeply psychotic person privately and made progress in gaining his trust until, in a conversation with his parents at the end of the visit, we began to talk about him as if he weren't there. The person looked hurt and abruptly sat down, and I realized that I had made a mistake and was insulting him. I immediately began talking directly to the person and crouched so that I was at eye level with him. The rest of the conversation then included him. This allowed me to maintain the tentative trust that had been developing.

In seeking to establish a connection with a person with schizophrenia, it is very important to see the good seed in the problems that trouble them. People with schizophrenia usually have legitimate concerns and mean well, but these concerns are often ignored or glossed over because they interfere with the discussion about the person's problems and need for medication. Ignoring the good seed will cause needless points of contention to form. This is because while the intent of the individuals trying to help people with schizophrenia will be to get them on medication, the intent of people with schizophrenia is to solve the real and symbolic problems that they are deeply concerned about. Ignoring these problems and insisting that the discussion be solely about behavior and medication is taken as interfering with these problems being solved.

People with schizophrenia will often have extreme solutions to legitimate problems that may be socially responsible but impractical. For example, some people I've worked with have been very concerned about ecology, and one person temporarily refused to drive or ride in cars. This was very frustrating to his parents, who lived outside of town and needed to drive the person to appointments. While this seemed irrational to his parents and counselors, it was only irrational from the point of view of helping the person over-come schizophrenia. From the point of view of staving off a worldwide ecological crisis-which was the concern of the person with schizophrenia-if everyone who had cars stopped using them in favor of bicycles and mass transit there could be much more hope for future generations. In working with his parents on this issue, I encouraged them to acknowledge the good seed in the problem and express their belief that ecological problems had to be resolved. After negotiating with their child on this issue, he agreed to ride in cars when necessary.

Recognizing real problems that the person is concerned about and the person's earnestness is crucial. By doing so, one connects to the person's rational core and returns dignity to the person-both in action and in the perceptions of those around the person. It also sets up the basis for understanding the concerns that are motivating the person.

Being aware of the core personality inside the delusional framework is also essential to connecting with the person and making him or her an ally in the return to sanity. The core personality is the person who exists under the illness, who is trying to make sense of the hallucinations and delusions, and who is trying to find solutions to problems and to heal the illness independently.

Even while in extreme psychosis, people with schizophrenia will show signs of seeking improvement. These signs will often be in the form of non-medical therapies aimed at alleviating the problems people perceive around them, including their own illness. When I was first contacted by the parents of one young man, the father told me that the person was trying to increase the vitamin B-complex in his diet (which is a suggested dietary step) and was asking for an old shed on their property to be turned into a small sweat lodge. The parents were complying with both requests. The sweat lodge helped alleviate tension for the entire family and became a meeting place for the person and myself as we discussed his private world. Initially, our meetings took place in the dark, and after months of meeting in this way, I was gladdened when the person suddenly began to meet me with the light on. This was an indication of trust and progress with his situation, and it was followed by substantial gains in his condition.

When the core person is contacted, people with schizophrenia will discuss real problems, sometimes personal, sometimes universal. As previously said, it is important not to minimize real problems, but rather to honestly discuss these situations and how the individual talking with the person with schizophrenia is trying in his or her own way to help alleviate the problem. As a result, the person who is intervening becomes more trustworthy to the person with schizophrenia.

In working with the core personality, it is important to explain that those who are concerned about the person with schizophrenia are hoping he or she will balance legitimate concerns with personal needs. Returning to the theme that the person with schizophrenia is a lovable and worthwhile person, the individual talking to the person with schizophrenia should discuss the possibility of using practical solutions rather than extreme solutions as a means of balancing needs.

It is crucial that no one say things like "Everything will be okay if you take medication" or "The world will be fine, stop worrying about it." This is simply untrue. Medication doesn't cure the world's woes or the real problems of the family and community that the person is concerned about. Few things are more damaging to dialogue with people with schizophrenia than choosing to gloss over their real concerns. Instead, it is important that helpers be willing to face the real problems people with schizophrenia are concerned about and listen respectfully to legitimate concerns.

I recall clearly an experience I had in this vein at two conferences on mental illness that I attended, one in the fall of 1999 and one in the fall of 2001. At both conferences, I discussed the importance of facing the real problems that people with schizophrenia are concerned about. In doing so, I said, "Don't just say to the person, 'Don't worry about the end of the world.'" In the second conference, which occurred a few weeks after September 11th, this statement was followed by a frightened silence in the room. I realized that many sane people in the room were concerned about the end of the world, some for the first time in their life. I made a mental note that people with schizophrenia are sometimes more aware of the extent of world problems than those around them, and therefore may seem like people crying wolf, except at times when the world's problems reach a crisis. From the viewpoint of many people with schizophrenia, the tendency of many ordinary people to ignore problems until they become crises makes extreme solutions the only alternative to disaster.

By following the steps discussed above, it is possible to calm a psychotic person and make him or her more flexible and willing to cooperate with others. After establishing this environment and soothing the person, further steps can be made to move the person toward stability, acceptance of diagnosis, and commitment to take medication. Even for those who show little improvement on medication, this approach can help create a happier psychosis, making the experience more positive for the person with schizophrenia and making him or her easier to work with.

Dealing with a Person in Crisis

When working with a person in crisis, there are a number of things that one can do to end the crisis successfully. Some of these techniques are simple and can be applied in most situations; others are more complex and can be used when no one involved is in immediate danger.

There are three rules that can be applied to most crises involving people with schizophrenia. The first is to remember that people with schizophrenia are emotional sponges. Calmness in the intervener will build calmness in the person in crisis. An example of this occurred when I saw a counselor talking to a person who was very angry. The person was yelling at the counselor, telling the counselor to leave him alone. The counselor responded by casually folding his arms, leaning against the wall of the house, and looking away momentarily as if distracted or bored. The counselor then replied calmly and simply. Within a minute, the person with schizophrenia was also leaning against the house, much calmer and cooler. He continued to calm down, and eventually agreed to meet with the counselor again.

A second simple rule is to never mention medication during a crisis. Mentioning medication to a person in crisis will cause paranoia to flare up. For that reason, it is better for family members and professionals to wait to discuss medication until after the crisis has subsided.

The third rule also relates to paranoia. If the person with schizophrenia exhibits paranoia toward the person doing the intervention, such as being frightened or hostile of all police, the best response is to deal with the problem on the individual level. Instead of saying that the person should trust police in general, respond with statements like "I'm a good guy who wants to help." This, along with a calm demeanor and interest in what the person in crisis is saying, helps the individual feel safer.

The more complex techniques for working with a person in crisis begin with remembering to look for the good seed in the problem. Crises are oftentimes attempts to symbolically and dramatically solve a problem, and people with schizophrenia will see interference with extreme or magical solutions as a sign that the other person is in favor of the problem getting worse. For example, if someone is causing a disruption by trying to get into a radio station to broadcast a warning in code that the end of the world is about to occur, those who attempt to stop him or her will be viewed as wanting the world to end.

To counteract this, it is important to recognize the perceived problem and express sympathy and a willingness to listen and help. Do not try to talk a person out of the delusions or minimize perceived or real problems. Instead, express concern for the person's well-being and for the world.

In the example of the person at the radio station, those responding to the situation should attempt to establish a dialogue to understand what the person thinks is going on and what he or she is trying to do. One should respond as if what the person with schizophrenia is saying may be plausible, explaining that one wants the world and the person with schizophrenia to be okay. Say things like, "It must be very hard on you to deal with this all alone," and "This is new to me. It would help me if I can understand what you see going on." Remaining calm and attentive helps the person with schizophrenia feel safe and that the individual responding is a potential ally.

If the individual who is intervening understands the point of view of the person with schizophrenia, it is helpful to step inside the delusional framework with "if" statements. If what you say is true, what about this? For example, I once met with a person in a crisis who told me that everyone was God except for him and that God wanted him to kill himself. He had cut himself a little and was saying that he had to kill himself. I responded that if everyone was a part of God, then I was part of God and I could tell him that God loved him, wanted him to live and be happy. After I worked with the person for about an hour or so, he calmed enough that he agreed to meet with his mental health workers and consider going to a three-day outpatient facility. A few days after that, he had a breakthrough where he decided to reject his voices and commit to taking medication.

Finally, it is important to be aware of the calm after the storm. Crises are caused by a slow buildup of adrenalin-like chemicals prior to the crisis. This buildup is expended in the crisis, and after crises have passed people are often more suggestible and willing to work with others. This is in part because they are at a lower level of chemical imbalance and also in part because what they expected to happen during the crisis didn't happen, causing a momentary questioning of some of their delusions. Since placing the person in a care facility will tend to result in a build-up of paranoia, this period will be brief. The best use of the time between the crisis and the renewed paranoia is to have family members and friends visit and express their concern for the person's well-being and the world.

Long-Term Approaches

In working with a psychotic individual, it is possible to stabilize the person even while he or she is psychotic through using a "mentor/realist" treatment team. The "realist" person or people on the team use therapy techniques such as Reality Therapy to advocate use of medication and facing problems created by the mental illness. The "mentor" uses therapy akin to Carl Roger's Client-Centered Therapy to gain the trust of the person in psychosis. This process is aimed at connecting with the individual's rational core within the delusional framework of schizophrenia and stabilizing the person through building trust and identifying real life issues.

To gain a person's trust, the mentor listens to the person's view of the world, allowing the person with schizophrenia to lead discussion and air concerns without being contradicted. The mentor seeks to have an understanding of the real and imagined issues of concern and supports the person when he or she is concerned about real issues. In the early phase, it is more important to develop trust and rapport than to seek changes in the person's viewpoint or behavior. It is vital for the mentor to show that he or she wants the person to be happy and wants positive resolutions of the person's concerns. It is essential not to make judgments, exert authority, or contradict the person with schizophrenia's view of reality.

As trust is built, people with schizophrenia will become calmer and exhibit more flexibility due to the discovery of an ally in the mentor. After reaching this point of trust, people will begin to express concerns about their life and the other issues that they are concerned about. The mentor should be supportive and encouraging when someone recognizes that his life needs help, and should act as a sounding board for the various alternative strategies the person devises for improving his life. The mentor should encourage the person to test the various strategies to see how well they work. The point is to create a safe environment where people with schizophrenia can acknowledge that they need to improve their lives.

As the person with schizophrenia attempts to stabilize without medication, the realist will be pushing for medication and concrete solutions. The mentor will act as advocate for the person's rational core, suggesting reasonable changes and responses in others to the real life issues that the person is concerned about. When the person's trust is strong enough and alternative solutions have been tested, the mentor gingerly suggests that medication may provide a solution. When this suggestion is made, the mentor always states that the choice to use medication is up to the person.

Eventually, the person with schizophrenia will decide to try medication as a solution. This is the next in a series of stages where the mentor continues to use this approach to progress through trying medication, stabilizing on medication, fully accepting diagnosis, sorting out delusions from accurate perceptions, and bringing the person back into mainstream society.

(A) Family, Friends, and Counselors - Setting up the Mentor/Realist Team

To deal with the person with schizophrenia in the long term, the people around the person with schizophrenia should set up a mentor/realist partnership. The roles of mentor and realist should be set up with family and possibly friends, fitting the personalities of the people around the person with the roles that best suit them. Ideally, the family and the mental health workers can co-ordinate multiple mentors and realists, with the various people playing their roles off each other. It is important to maintain private communication between the team members to compare notes, but the mentor(s) should also be careful to keep the secrets the person tells them unless someone's life is in danger. The trust between the person and the mentor is essential to the success of the approach.

During the process of treatment, the realist will push medication and other practical issues, while the mentor will attempt to listen, support, and seek underlying connections. The mentor will eventually be in a place to advise the others on approaches that the person with schizophrenia may respond to due to the beliefs and issues that underlie the confused communication. From the realist's perspective, the goal is for the person to take medication; from the mentor's perspective, the goal is for the family and the person to mutually resolve issues that are at the core of the person's distress.

If there is a single family caregiver, try to work out a similar relationship between the mental health workers and the caregiver. In most circumstances such as these, the family member will be the mentor. In these circumstances, it is essential that the single caregiver take part in a regular support group, such as the National Alliance on Mental Illness, and to have advanced treatment plans set up for probable crises.

(1) The Understanding Mentor

The purpose of the mentor is to reduce and eventually eliminate the paranoia that is central to schizophrenia. Central to this role will be the mentor acting as an advocate for both a peaceful and positive environment around the person and for the resolution of real-life issues that may be causing turmoil within or around the person. At the same time, it is crucial that the mentor never be in a position of authority over the person but, rather, be someone who can be thought of as an equal and an ally in the person's desire for a better life. This is aided by the mentor giving a copy of the essay in Appendix E to the person in psychosis once the treatment team agrees to do so. This essay was written in response to requests for material aimed at the person in psychosis.

The relationship between the mentor and the person mentored must go through several stages, just like a normal relationship between any two people. These stages are:

(1) Gaining trust and becoming a confidant.

(2) Listening to issues and providing support.

(3) Coming to understand the person's viewpoint.

(4) Helping the person recognize that his or her life is not working.

(5) Being a sounding board for alternative strategies for self-help and trying out the strategies.

(6) Gingerly suggesting medication when the person seems ready for the idea.

(7) Assisting with the transition to accepting diagnosis and medication.

During the initial meetings, it is important that the mentor focus on building trust. The mentor should let the person with schizophrenia lead the conversation, listen attentively, not contradict or ask leading question, and seek to understand and have compassion for what the person is going through. The purpose of the first stage in dealing with a psychotic person is not to alter behavior, but to give the person reasons to trust and like the counselor. As the person talks, it is important to reflect on what he or she seems to be saying and look to understand his or her perspective—even if it is wildly delusional.

Even though people with schizophrenia do not trust easily, they are also actively looking for allies in their real and imagined struggles. Since both real and imagined problems stem from the same reality, contradicting obviously delusional statements seems to the person with schizophrenia to be preventing solutions—including to the real problems. At the same time, finding people to listen to the delusional framework is fairly difficult. When a person takes time to listen and seeks to understand, the person with schizophrenia will usually appreciate the person and see him or her as a potential ally. This is the first step toward recovery—getting the person with schizophrenia to trust someone on the treatment team or in the circle of family or friends around him or her. Listening to the person with schizophrenia in a supportive manner is the crucial means by which trust is built.

When searching for literature that describes how to listen to a person with schizophrenia, counselors, family and friends should look into the approach of Carl Roger's Client-Centered Therapy. Using this approach, along with occasional reflecting and summarizing of what the person is saying, helps the person feel heard and safe. It is important when reflecting back what the person is saying that the confidant's tone and manner convey respect and seeking to understand. While the statements may seem wild or bizarre, it is helpful to treat them as important to understanding both what the person perceives and what the underlying problems in reality might be. This knowledge can be used to build the relationship with the person, indicating to others on the treatment team what the person is concerned about, and sets up an environment which will help calm the person.

As the mentor comes to understand the person's issues, these concerns can serve as the basis of building further trust. Finding positive concerns, such as ecological issues or desires for problem solving, allows the treatment team to show the person with schizophrenia that they share these concerns, helping alleviate the isolation and paranoia that the person feels. Doing these things will help the person be more malleable and cooperative with other aspects of his or her behavior.

While the mentor can convey concerns in general terms, it is important that the mentor actively maintains confidences that are revealed by the person with schizophrenia. The person will come to express deep feelings, fears, traumas, and wounds to the mentor. These personal facts and feelings must be kept in confidence unless someone's life is in danger. It is important that the mentor clearly state that he or she will keep the secrets and will only tell others something the person says if someone's life is in jeopardy. Establishing and following those ground rules allows trust to be built. The degree to which the mentor conveys the general outline of what the person says is a judgment call on that person's part, and should be made as if the person with schizophrenia were actually a good friend who considers the mentor a confidant. For the person with schizophrenia, that is exactly what the mentor will become, and this must be respected and appreciated.

In discussing what the person with schizophrenia talks about, it is helpful to use the concepts of "personal" and "consensus" reality. These concepts were first used with me while I was psychotic by a friend who wanted to acknowledge my thoughts as being valid to me but not what most people around me thought. In this perspective, the person with schizophrenia has unique experiences that make up his or her personal reality. This reality may contain many valid experiences and secrets along with delusions and false perceptions. At the same time, we all exist in a commonly defined reality—consensus reality—that may be at odds with personal reality. The person seeking to understand the person with schizophrenia wants to share personal reality with him or her and become a bridge between the two realities.

If the mentor finds that the person in psychosis reacts poorly to the terms personal and consensus reality, the words "experience" and "experiences" can be used in place of "reality." For some, hearing the terms "personal experience" and "consensus experience" is less judgmental than using the word reality. This suggestion was made to me by a woman who was working with her son and found that he reacted poorly to the word "reality" but reacted better to the word "experience."

Likewise, the mentor will want to interchange "hallucinations" with "visions" and make it clear to the person with schizophrenia that only time will make the difference clear between the two experiences. Visions will be accurate intuitions, whereas hallucinations will amount to static. While seeming to support the delusions of schizophrenia, this approach helps people with schizophrenia acknowledge that some of the experiences are valid—as they actually are—while others only cause confusion.

The focus of the mentor is not to inform a person with schizophrenia of reality, but rather to become a trusted person who can help create a calm center where it is possible to examine one's life. From that calm center, separating meaningful experiences from delusions and coming to recognize that one's life is not working is the mid-range goal of this approach. By connecting with people and offering a means to discuss experiences from a perspective that provides a middle-ground between delusional and realistic thinking, dialogue between people with schizophrenia and those around them can be opened up and progress toward alleviating paranoia can be made.

As the relationship between the person with schizophrenia and the mentor builds, the person will begin to discuss real problems and difficult events. As this happens, it is helpful not only to support the person but also to encourage the person to recognize that his or her life needs help. People with schizophrenia are very defensive about their ability to cope with reality, so it is best to not directly discuss problems unless the person brings them up. Instead, it is helpful to talk about how much happier people are "when their lives are working" and "when they are able to get what they want." When bad things happen, it is also helpful to express to the person that that the mentor is "sorry that you [the person with schizophrenia] had to go through that." Approaching sorrows and turmoil in a nonjudgmental, compassionate way helps people recognize that things could be better. This approach allows people with schizophrenia to realize and acknowledge that their lives are not working and they would be happier if things were different.

Once people with schizophrenia begin to discuss problems, they will also begin to discuss different ways to solve these problems. In many cases, these will be things that they had been trying to do before they began talking to the mentor and will range from realistic to delusional. As people confide in the mentor about what they are thinking of doing to help themselves, the mentor can become a sounding board for alternative strategies. It is important for the mentor to be open-minded, even to the point of discussing magic and other mind-over-matter means of improving the situation. As people relate possible solutions, the mentor should encourage them to try all safe possibilities, pointing out that it will become clear what works as time goes on.

Eventually, the person will seem ready for the idea that medication may provide a solution. This is best handled gingerly by the mentor. Ideally, the person will bring up the possibility on his or her own. As time goes on, the person will become more accepting of using medication and, after a while, will make a decision to take the medication.

It is important for the mentor to remember that ultimately the person with schizophrenia must make the decision that he or she wants to return to consensus reality. The mentor should approach the person from the philosophy that people with schizophrenia are choosing to be psychotic to achieve something deep within and around themselves and that the psychosis will have "run its course" when this deep change has occurred. For example, one person's commitment to take medication immediately followed his decision that he deserved to live. A second person's decision followed within a few months of his telling his mother that he had been molested by a brother as a child, a secret he had kept in his personal reality for over a decade.

As a final note, when choosing a mentor, it is important that the person not be a member of a group towards which the person with schizophrenia is hostile. Mentors benefit from having experience with hallucinations, such as people who have recovered from schizophrenia or people who have used hallucinatory drugs. Mentors also benefit from openness to a mystical viewpoint, with the attitude that when it comes to mystical events "the proof is in the pudding"—that only time will make it clear whether an intuitive experience or a hallucination has some basis in reality.

(2) The Consensus Realist

The "Realist" person or people assume the normal role of encouraging the person with schizophrenia to face the problems caused by the disease and to commit to using medicine to deal with the disease. A realist is able to react normally to the person and can lead conversations focused on problems, inappropriate behavior, real life difficulties, and so forth. The approach used by the realist is probably best described in the literature on Reality Therapy. However, there are special techniques and phrases that need to be applied when working with a person with schizophrenia.

It is the tendency for people in the realist role to focus attention on immediate acceptance of medical help and medication. For the person with schizophrenia, however, the problems do not appear to be medical, and since the typical realist reaction is to ignore and reject delusional statements, medical treatment takes on the appearance of interfering with the person's attempts to solve personal and world problems. For this reason, a conversation about the person's problems should include the phrases, "getting your life to work," "being able to get what you want out of life," and "being able to get what you need to be happy." While it is tempting to stress the use of medicine in seeking solutions to the person's problems, the most frequent statements by the realist should be "I am committed to your life working in whatever way it takes" and "I am committed to your happiness, whatever that takes." Then the suggestions of seeking medical help and taking medication will serve the purpose of letting the person know that the realists believe medical help is a good idea.

It is the natural impulse of family members and counselors to want to intervene and warn people when they see impending problems. Like someone watching a child sledding down a steep hill toward a tree, the realist will want to warn the child to watch out. What happens with people with schizophrenia, teenagers, and young adults, however, is that once they crash into the tree, they blame the person who warned them. From the viewpoint of the person with schizophrenia, if the realist hadn't interfered, he or she could have handled the situation without any problems.

For this reason, the treatment team should avoid warning people about problems they are likely to cause to themselves. After the problem has arisen, the treatment team can use the incident to help illustrate to the person that he or she needs help. This can be a very frustrating experience for the outsiders, but it is in the calm after the storm that people with schizophrenia will be more malleable and more willing to accept the possibility that their lives are not working. This is the first goal of the realist treatment team—to have the person recognize that his or her life is not working. Only after this has happened will the person accept the possibility that medical treatment may be a wise option.

When the realist is working with the person, it is important to respond in positive ways to real issues. Information from both the person's conversations with the realist and the mentor will help inform the treatment team's concerns. As with the mentor, it is important that the realist acts and speaks in ways that are allied with the person's concerns. Ideally, the realist will even alter some behavior to show responsiveness to the person with schizophrenia. For example, if the person with schizophrenia has concerns about the environment, family members could join a recycling program - a helpful way to ally themselves with the person and also have a positive impact in the real world on a real problem.

Realists often get stuck in a rut of criticizing numerous small problems associated with the person's behavior. This often interferes with discussion of the acute problems of schizophrenia by alienating the person unnecessarily. For that reason, it is best to limit criticisms of harmful behavior as much as possible. By focusing on concerns about harmful and risky behavior, ineffective arguments about less dangerous behavior are avoided. The focus also allows the realist to make it clear to the person that the realist is especially concerned with the person's health and well-being, and is particularly concerned about behavior that is a danger to the individual or someone else. This focus helps the person make clear distinctions about what is expected and what is not, and helps the person understand why the realist is concerned about his or her life.

When discussing problems caused by the person with schizophrenia, it is helpful to discuss the behavior in light of the person's concerns. For example, one person was concerned about the environment but would fly into panicked rages and break objects in the home. The breaking of things appeared to be an attempt by the person to protect himself from voices. I encouraged the person's parent to point out that by breaking things the person was wasting the resources that had been used to make the objects, thus harming the environment. For that reason, it would be helpful to the environment if the person could find a non-destructive means of accomplishing whatever he was trying to do. This gave the person food for thought and helped him approach the place where he realized that he needed help.

Finally, it is important to illustrate concerns by pointing out situations where the person with schizophrenia is asking for special treatment while claiming to be normal. The realist can point out ways that the person is requesting or demanding that he or she be treated as privileged, such as being a young adult allowed to live at home without rent or a job, while also claiming to be normal. By doing so, the realist can focus the person's thinking on the contradiction between claims of normalcy and actual behavior.

The eventual goal of getting people with schizophrenia to take medication can be helped by approaching them in these ways. Prior to accepting medication, people with schizophrenia must come to understand that their lives are not working and that they need help. By following the guidelines above, the realist treatment team can help move people with schizophrenia toward this acceptance with a minimum amount of alienation or increase in paranoia.

(B) Other Aspects of Long Term Treatment

(1) The Plateau/Crisis Cycle

During psychosis, the person with schizophrenia goes through a frustrating roller-coaster ride of stabilizing at a plateau and then falling into a crisis that results in hospitalization. After a period of being hospitalized, the person seems well enough to be released, after which he or she returns to their plateau, only to deteriorate again into another crisis and another hospitalization. For family and friends, this is an extremely difficult time, since there seems to be no hope of recovery. Even times of stability are deceiving, since they are followed by crisis.

The cycle that is commonly experienced has aspects that explain why things happen the way they do. After initial hospitalization, people with schizophrenia realize that we are locked into a very unpleasant environment because people think we are crazy. Unless we are highly psychotic, we are able to see those aspects of our behavior that are perceived as schizophrenic. We recognize that others think we are crazy, but accurate intuitions and other real and symbolic events give us reason to think that we are experiencing a reality that others are blind to and that they misinterpret as insane.

Since we want out of the hospital, we decide we they will simply stop the behavior that people think of as crazy. We stop telling people about our experiences, claim to no longer believe what we still actually believe, and secretly harbor our delusions. To outsiders, we have improved, but in fact we have only improved enough to fake the behavior that others desire for us. We are released from the hospital with bitter feelings toward those around us, eager to resume our quest for mystical understandings and miraculous solutions to personal and world problems. We stop taking medication, become secretive, and begin the slow descent toward a new crisis.

The problem of harboring delusions creates a huge difficulty for the normal approach to dealing with schizophrenia. When we begin to hide our symptoms, outsiders lose contact with our rational core and opportunities to observe and help us are lost until the next crisis erupts. Our paranoia becomes more powerful and our trust of family and friends is lost. The medical establishment, with their locked doors and powerful drugs, become the enemy that is stopping us from achieving our goal of miraculous solutions to huge problems.

In this setting, the role of the mentor becomes very helpful. People with schizophrenia begin to assign good and bad roles to people, with those seeking to give them medication seen as bad and those who will listen to their delusions and not call them crazy seen as good. The mentor is someone that the person with schizophrenia is hoping to find, an ally in the quest toward personal and world salvation. If the mentor is successful, soon after first meeting, the person will begin to pour out the delusions that he or she has been harboring and begin to talk about hallucinatory experiences. This is, in fact, the first step toward complete trust and eventual recovery.

During these initial phases, the person with schizophrenia may want the mentor to experiment with magical solutions. This is harmless, since the solutions will probably not consistently work, and thus will provide evidence to contradict the delusions over time. For example, once when I first contacted a person with schizophrenia, he told me that he was seeking to learn how to control the weather to save the world from global warming. He wanted to see if he could use his mind to split clouds in two, since he had heard that this was possible. He asked me to help him. I agreed, silently hoping that the clouds would remain stable. We sat outside, and tried to split clouds, and failed. As a result, he saw that he could trust me to experiment with magical solutions. Furthermore, since I never mentioned the incident to his parents or anyone else, he learned he could trust me with secrets. Once we were past this phase of trust building, I could play a more helpful role in interpreting his behavior for his parents, and helping him remain calm during our visits.

(2) Synchronicity - Thinking like a Person with Schizophrenia

In working with a person with schizophrenia, it is helpful to think about mystical concepts, like believing that everything happens for a reason, coincidences having special meaning, and about synchronicities like intuition and prophetic dreams. These concepts underlie many real and imagined experiences. They describe the reality that people with schizophrenia witness. Whether others wish to believe that there is a basis for these beliefs or not, becoming familiar with this kind of thinking is helpful in understanding the person with schizophrenia.

Reading books like Jung's *Symbols of Man* and the fiction *Celestine Prophecy* are ways to become familiar with some of the thinking that people with schizophrenia develop. While one may disagree with the mystical mindset found in this literature, it is important not to attempt to argue people out of their beliefs. The mystical frame of mind accurately depicts the experiences that people have, and arguing against this perspective alienates people with schizophrenia. Reviewing the appendices on hallucinations can give the reader a sense of the experiences people with schizophrenia have. Given these experiences, the reader can hopefully understand how the person naturally develops mystical thinking.

(3) Recognizing the Good Seed - Negotiating Core Beliefs to Be Saved

The medical team, family and friends should see their interactions with the person with schizophrenia as negotiating what beliefs can be retained once the person accepts his or her diagnosis. For people with schizophrenia, accepting diagnosis means surrendering the right to define reality for themselves and turning over their freedom of thought to others. This is a major commitment, one which few sane adult people would do willingly.

To expedite this process, it is important to see the good seeds at the core of the person's beliefs, acknowledging them, and recognizing their validity. As the person's key positive beliefs are accepted by the treatment team, the individual's paranoia is reduced and he or she become less apprehensive about turning over control of his or her thinking to others.

Often the key to recovery will lie in people with schizophrenia revealing secrets or dealing with intensive inner turmoil that lies at the heart of their double binds and dilemmas. As time goes on, providing a safe place for this inner turmoil to be brought to the surface will serve as the basis for lasting stability and long-term recovery.

(4) Medication and Alternatives

It is important to be aware that there are alternatives to medication that can be successful in alleviating the symptoms of psychosis. A failure of the first edition of this handbook was to ignore this fact. There are in fact three general treatment modalities for psychosis: no need for medication, medication being necessary and successful (which is my situation) and medication having only limited success. Essential to the success of alternatives to medication is the resolving of the person's internal and external conflicts. In my mind this is an approach where applying the material in the chapter on "Counseling for Self-Understanding" is done during psychosis and, as with Open Dialogue approach, there is a seeking resolution with people around person as well. The choice of medication verses not using medication is discussed in detail in the second half of the following chapter.

For those who want to apply the material in this book without pushing medication, I suggest that they create the mentor/realist team as suggested, but the stages for the understanding mentor end differently. In the beginning of the section on the understanding mentor, stage 6 involved the suggesting medication and stage 7 followed up on this stage. In place of that, those who do not wish to push medication should have a stage 6 in which the mentor convey to the person in psychosis that they may be hallucinating. As the process of explaining that the person is hallucinating unfolds, the mentor will want to have the person review the reality checking rules in the chapter on "Stabilizing on Medication" and negotiate agreements on how the person can check their experiences to confirm that they are or are not occurring in consensus reality. Once reality checking habits are established, the mentor and the person in psychosis can move into the material on "Counseling for Self-Understanding" and seek to unwind the inner turmoil that is projected into the hallucinations and delusions of the person. As this process happens, the realist members of the team would push for resolution of real-life problems caused by misperception of events. It is important that the realists do not push for solutions in such a way that they actually exacerbate the tension within the person, but rather seek to remind the person of the need to deal with the outside world as it becomes possible. Assuming the treatment team agrees, the realists do not have to push for the use of medicine.

It should be noted that this alternative approach can be used for people who are using medication but who continue to have some symptoms, including hallucinations and voices. At the same time, I recommend that those who are committed to not pushing medication observe how well the person progresses without medication. Being committed to a single approach—whether it is medication without counseling or alternative approaches without medication—fails to provide a diversity of options for the person in psychosis and thereby limits the potential number of solutions available.

CHAPTER THREE
STABILIZING ON MEDICATION

Stabilizing on medication, like the cycle of plateau and crisis, is often a series of repeated steps during which people with schizophrenia learn to recognize their disease and develop strategies for coping with their experiences. Stabilization often occurs during the last cycles of plateau and crisis. After the mentor has established trust, and the person and the mentor are having discussions about the problems in the person's life, it is possible for the mentor to discuss the need for the person "to return to consensus reality." This is done in part by pointing out that even while people may be experiencing a personal reality, they are also part of consensus reality, and need to be able to separate experiences that are unique to them from experiences that are shared by everyone. Once this discussion is begun, the mentor can help the person realize when he or she is experiencing things that are not part of consensus reality and are considered by others to be psychotic.

As this discussion continues over time, people with schizophrenia will begin to discuss their hallucinations, voices, and delusions in their own terminology, similar to the parallel meanings of vision and hallucination and personal and consensus reality. The mentor will link the way the person is thinking of his or her disease with the way that the realist thinks of the disease, using that as a basis for showing the person over time that these experiences are interfering with his or her happiness and keeping life from working out.

In doing these steps, the mentor and realist treatment team is working to help the person recognize his or her disease as such. People with schizophrenia will believe that the hallucinatory episodes are showing them a reality behind the reality commonly observed, and will point to real intuitive experiences that support this belief. It is helpful for the mentor to recognize when accurate intuition has occurred, but at the same time to discuss with the person the fact that many of these experiences may simply be "static" that is nonsense or misinformation. As the person's experiences proceed, he or she will see this to be true. Many of these experiences do not seem easily understood, and some will be very unpleasant. As time continues, many people with schizophrenia will grow to realize that they are experiencing events that fit the category of hallucination and these experiences are interfering with their life.

It might appear that the process being described is a lengthy one and one which might be slower than simply attempting to force the person to take medication. Instead, the dialogue established by the mentor simply recognizes that the time between diagnosis and commitment to take medication is a lengthy one and attempts to reach the rational core and have him or her become part of the process of recovery. The process of working with the psychotic person is helped by the calming influence of the mentor and allows for longer periods of plateau and more substantial cooperation on the part. The mentor/realist approach also makes the acceptance of diagnosis easier on the person and lessens some of the post-traumatic effects of psychosis.

As the treatment team and the person with schizophrenia work to recognize the various aspects of the disease, dialogues will begin on the voices and hallucinations and what the individual can do to deal with these events. Helping the person develop a response to these events, even while he or she is somewhat psychotic, is a means of forging an alliance between the treatment team and the person. They will be working collectively on the experiences to help lessen the impact of events in his or her personal reality. As this process continues, people will be developing skills for dealing with their disease well into the future.

A key practice to encourage is reality checking, a plan of action that involves asking a trusted person to verify whether or not something which may be a hallucination or delusional thought seems accurate. For example, when someone behind the person with schizophrenia makes a noise and no one seems to notice, it is a good practice for the person to ask if someone really did make a noise. As people with schizophrenia become more aware of their experiences, reality checking can serve to highlight potential problems and indicate the possible need to increase or change medication. It can also serve to help the person learn to separate hallucinatory experiences from those in consensus reality.

As reality checking continues, it is helpful to have the mentor discuss the need to rely on other trusted people to define reality. This applies not only to ongoing experiences, but also to the ideas that the person with schizophrenia has been developing in his/her personal reality. This is an important and lasting phase of early recovery, and one in which the responsibilities of those defining the reality cannot be understated. The person with schizophrenia will naturally have questions about spirituality, religion, psychic phenomenon, politics, and many other controversial topics. The difficult responsibility of the people being trusted to define reality is to honestly answer not only their personal beliefs, but also with the beliefs of others who are in the range of normal, functioning people.

People with schizophrenia will have superstitious and sometimes seemingly bizarre beliefs arising from their experiences. The natural impulse of those around the person is to reject these beliefs outright in fear of losing contact with reality. Approaching the process of defining reality evenhandedly is important, however. One should especially consider if the belief seems to be hampering the recovery, and to proceed from the practical and honest point of view of what is helpful for the person. Being willing to split hairs, discuss philosophy, and entertain beliefs far from one's own perspective is important to being fair to people with schizophrenia. As a result, people with schizophrenia will be able to strengthen their trust in the people around them and bring to light many aspects of their personal realities.

After the person has clearly accepted his/her diagnosis and is in dialogue about the disease with the mentor, it is helpful for the mentor to work with the person on rules for reality checking. This process is to provide the guidelines which people must apply for the rest of our lives. While foreign to normal thinking, their application to someone who might have hallucinations at any time is clear.

(1) Nothing that happened during psychosis is known to have happened for certain.

(2) Nothing that happens when alone is known to have happened for certain.

(3) Anything odd that happens when alone should be discussed with others as a possible hallucination and then ignored.

(4) Anytime people have a possible hallucination they should check reality with someone else present.

(5) Anytime people are alone and a possible hallucination occurs, they should test reality as insofar as possible. For example, once when I was alone a radio seemed to suddenly come on and play a song, then stop. I went to the radio and turned it on and heard a news program, deducing that I had just hallucinated.

(6) Any hallucination should be reported and possible changes in medication discussed.

(7) Anything that is considered a possible hallucination, including experiences during psychosis, should eventually be explored as symbolic experiences with personal meaning. The goal of the new approach to reality for the person should be "I may not know if something happened, but I know what it signified to me."

After people with schizophrenia have accepted diagnosis and begun to apply the reality checking and have started allowing others to define their reality, it is important to discuss early warning signs and sources of stress. To do this, it is necessary for the treatment team and the person to review the events of psychosis and find what symptoms occurred prior to the cyclic crises. Most people's early warning signs will include insomnia, irritability, and beliefs that they have discovered a miraculous solution to difficult problems. They will also include more individual symptoms. One of my early warning signs is that I will hear marching bands when none are playing.

Along with the development of agreed upon early warning signs, there is also a need to identify sources of stress and to find ways to minimize these factors. Most modern lifestyles contain numerous sources of stress, and building relaxation and protection from stress into both the life and the family will at first seem difficult, but later will be helpful to all involved. Once stress has been minimized, looking ahead for future sources of stress and preparing for the possibility of renewal of symptoms is a good practice. Simply keeping in mind that a person needs to nurture oneself in the face of stress is helpful in preventing reoccurrences. Having a Wellness Recovery Action Plan (WRAP) is also a wise way to prepare for possible difficulties.

As early recovery takes hold, another important step is for people with schizophrenia to expand the number of people they trust. They must begin to discuss their experiences during psychosis. This allows people with schizophrenia to more thoroughly understand what they have been through and the difference between hallucinations, voices, and normal reality.

It is also important that people with schizophrenia begin to share their delusions with others. The process of unlearning delusions is usually a very lengthy process, sometimes lasting over a decade. During this time it is important for people to discuss the delusions and themes of their mental illness and see if their beliefs still seem to hold water. In some cases, there will be beliefs that have some merit, though perhaps not in the way that the person first thought, while there may be others that are rejected completely.

A final challenge in early recovery is the tendency for people with schizophrenia to use recreational drugs. While some people can continue to use drugs and alcohol after initial recovery, many people have significant difficulty with drug use. Despite this, people do tend to want to party and will frequently have friends who do so. Adopting a process of keeping the person aware of how partying affects symptoms is important. At the same time, the opportunity for the person with schizophrenia to party is fairly common, and family members and counselors must be aware that it is ultimately the person with schizophrenia who will have to recognize the negative effects of partying on his/her recovery.

In some instances, it will be necessary for the person with schizophrenia to join a dual diagnosis group that supports recovery from co-occurring mental illness and drug addiction. While this is not necessary in all cases, dual diagnosis groups can serve as a means to gain the will to resist partying and thereby remain healthy.

Medication and Alternatives in the United States

The issue of using medication verses not using medication is a hotly debated topic at the present time. For me, the debate as it is presently being conducted is somewhat counter-productive for four reasons.

(1) Medication almost certainly limits or completely eliminates hallucinations and voices and is therefore needed with some people to alleviate symptoms.

(2) Medication alone is clearly ineffective in many situations to allow for full recovery and transformation of the person's life and is likewise not needed at all by some people.

(3) Proponents of medications and proponents of not using medication are oftentimes generalizing what works in some situations to be what should be done in all situations, rather than seeking to find common ground with each other.

(4) As a result of this controversy, many complementary approaches which can be combined with medication when medication is needed are unfairly polarized around the two extremes of medication-and-nothing-else and anything-but-medication. These two extremes do not serve the vast majority of people with schizophrenia, who vary tremendously from each other in what is needed to fully regain and transform our lives.

Treating schizophrenia with alternatives to medication and not using medication for all of one's life are possible as long as the paranoia and delusions that prompt harm to the person and others are dissolved. The different approaches outside of medication alone are similar to the treatment of diabetes or high cholesterol with diet and exercise alone. It should be noted that unlike diabetes or high cholesterol, experiences in psychosis, when carefully approached and integrated into one's life, can have positive effects (See the chapter on "Counseling for Self-Understanding" for one approach to this). It is also important to keep in mind that even when medication is required that some sort of complementary approach, ranging from counseling to meditation to dietary changes to substantial lifestyle changes, is always required. Just as treatment of diabetes and high cholesterol with medication alone is unwise, treatment of schizophrenia with medication alone is not very effective. Instead, it is best to focus on the commonly-recognized typology of three: Some people do not require medication to stem symptoms; some have almost all or all of their symptoms abated through medication; some have limited abatement of symptoms on medication. Seeking to treat people with schizophrenia with that in mind is helpful in being aware of alternatives.

At present there are a number of complementary approaches that can be used in working with people with schizophrenia: Cognitive Behavioral Therapy (CBT), Listen-Empathize-Agree-Partner (LEAP), the approach suggested in this handbook and Open Dialogue are all means to establish dialogues with the person who is hallucinating. Dr. Pat Deegan's CommonGround software and Personal Medicine are also very useful. Practitioners, family members and friends should become familiar with all of them and see them as complementary tools in a toolkit. The different techniques should be used as best fits the situation. Looking honestly at the available resources and family and community situations around the person are essential to mapping out a successful strategy for recovery. While some techniques will work in some situations, these same techniques may be very counterproductive in other situations. Being flexible and going with what works well for the individual situation is the key to success.

Open Dialogue, which is an approach from Western Lapland (Northern Finland), has high rates of recovery and is in the very earliest stages of possibly being introduced in the United States. This approach seeks intensive individual and group counseling in the home and community to alleviate symptoms and return the person to normal functioning. Medication is prescribed only when other alternatives have clearly failed. I am personally sympathetic to the Open Dialogue approach and look at it as potentially a very useful technique. It seems from my perspective to seek to achieve the goals of the chapter on "Counseling for Self-Understanding" with both the person and those around them during the psychosis, and thereby aims at a group transformation of turmoil.

Even so, I am skeptical that Open Dialogue can be easily transplanted to the United States. It is important to recognize that there is a marked lack of resources devoted to counseling services in this country. Given the present slashing of funds for these crucial services and the US culture's reliance on medication over changes in lifestyle for almost all health-related challenges, I am doubtful that even the most devoted activists and the most compelling evidence for the validity of the Open Dialogue approach will soon be able to bring the funding dollars needed to provide these services.

The Western Lapland area is also markedly different in history and culture than the United States. In Western Lapland there is a continuity of communities and families who have many centuries of a largely harmonious collective history, whereas the United States is a society mainly of immigrants with a distinct lack of continuity in our communities and families. Likewise, I suspect that the culture in Western Lapland emphasizes an importance of fitting together and sharing a collective identity, whereas the United States culture tends to have an individualistic focus and an emphasis on who's right and who's to blame. Our history is also marked by European invasions of the land, subjugation of native peoples and Africans, wars of expansion into land held by Mexico and Spain, an extremely bloody civil war, and by legacies of marked divisions in race, class, politics, regions, and creeds. These factors, which may not be pleasant for us to recognize, create an antagonism in our communities which make the sort of flexibility of identity required by Open Dialogue more difficult to attain. At the same time, our families are likewise marked by high rates of conflict and divorce, narcissism, borderline personality disorder, abuse, addictions, and other factors which make alleviation of symptoms through Open Dialogue less likely. While it is unfair to say these factors create mental illness, the combination of the lack of counseling resources and the lack of unity and flexibility in our communities and families are likely to limit the availability and effectiveness of the Open Dialogue approach in the United States for the foreseeable future.

Returning to the possible use of medication, there are two crucial questions to be examined to determine if the person in psychosis can resolve his or her challenge without medication.

(1) Can stresses and underlying conflicts, both inside and outside the person, be resolved enough that the hallucinations end and delusions can be unwound?

(2) Does the person exhibit signs of diminishing hallucinations and other symptoms when stress levels are low?

If the answer to either of these questions is no, medication is often necessary to stem the symptoms.

At the same time, it is important to recognize that in some cases, events akin to psychosis have had positive effects. For example, there are ample cases of lucid and sometimes very popular material derived from spontaneous speech attributed to spiritual entities, ranging from the 7th century Qur'an to the contemporary New Age Orin and DaBen series. Likewise, extraordinary achievements in hallucinatory states are matters of fact, including Sitting Bull's prophetic vision during the Lakota Sun Dance ceremony of the Lakota victory over Custer's forces and Pittsburgh Pirates pitcher Dock Ellis's no hitter in 1970 that Ellis pitched while on LSD. However, although these events indicate positive effects from altered states, it is crucial to understand that maintaining the health and wellbeing of the person experiencing them is central. The question is not simply are these experiences sometimes valid—they certainly can be—but do they also move the life, health, and well-being of the person forward? If not—as is often the case—the symptoms are best abated by some means.

It is also important to remember that once a person is on medication, careful steps to withdraw slowly from medication should be pursued if the person wishes to do so. To suddenly stop using antipsychotic medication can result in reoccurrence of symptoms, especially if underlying turmoil and tensions have not been resolved. For that reason, any decision to withdraw from medication requires a slow stepping down of dosage and regular evaluations to determine if the person is ready for the next reduction.

CHAPTER FOUR
REVIEWING POSSIBLE CAUSES
OF SCHIZOPHRENIA

At this point in this short book, we have moved from the horrifying realization that a family member is insane through cycles of extreme psychosis and crisis into the beginning stages of recovery. The past few pages have covered a timeframe which, in the most fortunate circumstances, will last two to three years, and in most cases will be longer. At this point in recovery, the family and friends are exhausted, the person with schizophrenia has a fragile hold on reality, and the future is uncertain. In these circumstances, the person with schizophrenia is normally on some sort of disability, either living in the family home or in special housing, and is suffering from post-psychotic trauma.

In many cases, people do not proceed much farther on the road toward recovery than this. We remain listless, unsure of ourselves, and are unable or unwilling to take the necessary steps toward regaining a mostly normal life. I personally believe that many people with schizophrenia can return to mainstream society and live a life as full as or fuller than most non-schizophrenic people. The key is for the person with schizophrenia, once fully stabilized and observing the rules of perception for a person with schizophrenia, to review his or her psychosis and come to grips with the inner turmoil and confusion that marked that period of time. To do this it is necessary to examine the possible causes of schizophrenia to arrive at a clearer understanding of the relationship between the psychosis and the reality.

My review of these ideas is not to argue that one possibility covers all the cases of schizophrenia that exist. Instead, it is to suggest that each possibility may be the cause of some of the cases a person with schizophrenia encounters. To argue that there is a single cause of schizophrenia which can be applied to all people is to get involved in what to me is mainly an ego game between ideas. It falls into the trap of believing that one's pet theory, whatever it is, is the only correct explanation and the pet theories of everyone who disagrees are wrong. I believe that when a person with schizophrenia walks into a hospital for treatment, there is no real way for the treatment team to determine what actually caused the schizophrenia. Over time, it is possible to make guesses about possible causes for that individual person, but making blanket statements about the causes of all cases of schizophrenia oversimplifies a very complex disease. It can also potentially eliminate treatments that might be very helpful in helping the person recover. For that reason, the suggested causes below should each be taken as one possible cause and each case should be examined for which cause or causes seem to be most likely true in that instance.

Case I: Genetic Determinism

The first possible cause of schizophrenia is that there is a gene which causes the disease. In this scenario, schizophrenia is an inherited trait that has been passed on through generations. The argument for this possibility is two-fold. Since schizophrenia can be treated by chemical therapy, it is likely to have a physical basis in the body, and since schizophrenia has been found to be more likely in children of people with schizophrenia, there is the probability that it is inherited.

There are examples of identical twins, however, where one twin has schizophrenia and the other twin doesn't. This indicates that in some cases, there must be environmental factors, ranging from diseases to psychological stresses, which may trigger schizophrenia. It is possible there is a genetic potential for schizophrenia that comes into being only when environmental stress reaches a certain level.

Case II: Extreme Trauma

When one becomes familiar with the stories of mentally ill people, some of these stories of the early lives of patients are horrifying. In my own experience, I have heard people with schizophrenia and other mentally ill people recount childhoods of such extreme abuse and trauma that merely hearing about them was nearly overwhelming. I have heard people recount unspeakable abuse that would damage the mental health of any normal adult person and obviously did horrific harm to the health of the child. In these cases, there is ample reason to believe that these children were literally driven insane by the abuse they received.

In working with these unfortunate people, medicine can often help them regain some measure of sanity. It is crucial, however, that their personal suffering be recognized and healed in some way. Treating victims of extreme trauma with medicine alone is ineffective and fails to recognize their needs as survivors of tremendous hardship.

Case III: Sensitive Person in a Brutal World

In the third case, there is a combination of personality and environment that results in the individual losing touch with reality. This combination, which seems fairly common among the people with schizophrenia I have known, is one where the person is a sensitive person, somewhat dreamy and artistic, and encounters trauma that he/she cannot cope with successfully. The source of the trauma may be from inside the family, or may be from community and other sources. I believe that this is the case that accounts for my schizophrenia.

It is important to note that the amount of trauma the person encounters may not be outside the range of normality. For example, it is conceivable that a person might come from a family where one or both parents are mildly alcoholic, or where the father is a veteran with severe emotional trauma from war, or where the parents are in conflict but decide to remain married for the sake of the children. All of these families fall well within the range of normal trials and tribulations of life, yet these conditions of long-standing and unresolved emotional pain may serve as the center for turmoil for a person with a sensitive and vulnerable personality. While other people would be able to retain a fairly healthy mental outlook, this person cannot resolve these issues. To achieve progress, it is essential that these issues be brought to the surface and some form of a resolution be made, even though the problems within the person's family and community may be less severe than the problems of the family and community of the psychiatrist or the counselors.

It is important to understand the way in which a dreamy or artistic personality combines with the emotional turmoil surrounding a person to create the core psychological issues a person must deal with. In the case of the schizophrenia peer group I worked with, the majority of us are men who are artistic in some way, such as playing musical instruments, sculpting clay, or writing prose and poetry. In many of our cases, our childhoods involved sustained exposure to alcoholism, abuse, incest, or some other combination of trauma that clearly affected us. Resulting from this combination we developed double binds, wounds, and secrets that increasingly plagued our lives and from which we attempted to escape through art and imagination. We began to turn to magical means to escape our lives, and through misunderstanding of mystical events, we lost touch with reality.

It cannot and should not be said that the problems around us resulted in our becoming schizophrenic. It must be said, however, that this is the description of the descent into insanity for us and to fully recover from the trauma of insanity, the issues of family, community, and worldwide problems must be recognized and in some way healed and resolved. For the people who fall into this category of causation, progress requires a resolution of severe problems in our past and sometimes present lives.

Case IV: Other Possibilities

In considering the possible causes of schizophrenia, it is important not to rule out less common sources. The possibility of a virus, some form of brain damage, or other sources of harm should be considered. If a person does not seem to have many environmental stresses or trauma and does not have a history of mental illness in the family, other possible sources should be considered. In the treating of schizophrenia, it is important to think of a variety of means to control the disease as best as possible.

An example of an unusual solution to schizophrenia is found in the autobiographical work by Carol North, M.D., *Welcome Silence.* In this case, the author is a psychiatrist and a former person with schizophrenia who was cured by dialysis, an experimental treatment that is no longer in use. In this case, the symptoms of schizophrenia were apparently caused by impurities in the woman's blood. Just as this rare case was solved by a means that was generally unsuccessful for others, it is worthwhile to explore all options. Assuming that a case of schizophrenia was caused by one factor instead of another should only proceed if treatment is working based on that assumption.

As long as the person with schizophrenia is suffering from the illness, the treatment team should consider all possible means to alleviate the problems caused by the illness.

CHAPTER FIVE
COUNSELING FOR SELF-UNDERSTANDING

At the present time, counseling for post-psychotic people is both insufficiently prescribed and tends to avoid delving deeply into issues of past trauma and their relationship to the delusions and hallucinations during psychosis. All too often, the advances in medication have been paired with a lost focus on counseling for people with schizophrenia, leaving many people with unresolved issues and trauma. After years of struggle to restore the person to some grip on reality, the drive for further advancement is lost. As a result, people with schizophrenia are frequently left to deal with the troubling issues of their life on their own.

Counseling for post-psychotic people is as essential as medication. Medication, in fact, is being shown to not always be needed, but some sort of review of experiences and re-orienting of one's life is essential. To counsel a post-psychotic person, it can be helpful to follow the guidelines discussed below to move the person with schizophrenia from confusion and vulnerability to clarity, renewed insight and personal strength. If counseling is successful, the person will have a better understanding of self and the people around him or her than most non-mentally ill people who have never received counseling.

Counseling and Group Counseling

After the person has clearly accepted diagnosis and committed to taking medication, the initial few months of counseling will be focused on the individual's new perspective and dealing with issues of facing life as a person with schizophrenia. As time passes, the person will be more able to reflect on his/her experiences during psychosis. This reflection is greatly aided by one-on-one and group counseling. The purpose of the counseling will be first to establish the rules of perception for schizophrenia and to restore some sense of calm and stability to the life and his or her family. After this phase, counseling can move forward to more complex issues.

Private counseling is important to allow the person to begin to talk about issues that he or she may be unable to discuss with others, including family and friends. The person or people who played the role of the mentor during psychosis will be in the most trusted position to be the counselor, but the mentor may not actually be a professional counselor. Even if the mentor is not a professional counselor, he or she should continue to be in contact with the person for several years after the return to sanity. During this time the mentor should expect and encourage the person to discuss his or her experiences during psychosis and any possible linkages between the real life of the individual and his or her hallucinations and delusions.

Counselors, both professionals and the mentor(s), should be prepared to work through a number of phases in early recovery. One of these is a tendency on the part to be naïve and gullible. Schizophrenia is marked by a focus on grand ideas about spirituality, life, reality, and other abstract thoughts. Returning to the mundane and everyday world causes confusion in people with schizophrenia, who will often attempt to understand daily events in terms of their universal significance. While many of these high-level ideas will seem nonsensical or overly idealistic to outsiders, the ideas of people with schizophrenia are the first attempts to link their experiences during psychosis with the reality of their lives. These ideas will be very important to people in recovery, because they represent their first attempts to bring intuitive and personal insights during psychosis into their daily lives. Counseling to link the grand ideas of people with schizophrenia to their personal lives and showing how these grand ideas have personal meaning to the individual is an important part of the transition to normal thinking. Attempting to show people that what applies to them and their personal lives may not apply to others is more difficult. This may require patience on the part of counselors, and should be approached from the perspective that as long as people with schizophrenia are not displacing anger or displaying hostility toward innocent people, the larger ideas of their philosophy should be respected as a personal choice. It is important not to push people with schizophrenia in early recovery too far in challenging their beliefs, as these beliefs contain the seeds of their new identity.

While in early recovery people with schizophrenia are often naïve and gullible while interacting with others. Subtle shades of meaning, such as sarcasm, double-entendre, exaggeration, and numerous other common means of expression are often lost on an individual newly restored to sanity. As a result, people will be prone to misunderstanding the ideas of others, often taking seriously statements and actions that have no serious intent. People with schizophrenia may take things to heart that are not meant to be taken seriously, or which are more the bravado and exaggeration of everyday talk than anything else. We are also vulnerable to predation from unkind people who will take advantage of our gullibility for their personal gain. For that reason, it is wise in the first couple of years of early recovery to maintain a relatively protected environment for people with schizophrenia and to keep an ongoing dialogue with us about our daily interactions with people.

People who are post-psychotic are prone to depression. It is important to keep an eye out for this and find means to reduce it if it occurs. When we wake up to our reality in early recovery, there are a number of shocks, ranging from the trauma of the psychotic experience and accepting our vulnerability, to facing a life situation which may be far worse than when we first developed symptoms. We are often impoverished, on disability, and facing a long, challenging road to regain the life that many normal people in industrialized countries take for granted. Facing the challenges of our new life is daunting, especially when linked with the devastating blows to our self-confidence that occurred after the recognition that we cannot trust our own perceptions.

Moving forward after returning from psychosis requires regaining our sense of reality and discovering that we can achieve things despite our illness. While we may initially believe that our life will never be the same, patiently taking a step-by-step approach to returning to a normal life is really the key. As time passes and we are able to accomplish things for ourselves, a renewed sense of confidence is attained and the risk of depression lessens. This, however, will often take years to be accomplished.

Sorting Through Delusions/Hallucinations for Accurate Insights/Accurate Intuition

The counseling described above is fairly common for people who are emerging from psychosis. What is uncommon, but very important, is going over the experiences during psychosis and sorting out the false beliefs and hallucinations from the accurate insights and authentic intuition. This is a very complex process. For most counselors, the idea there can be accurate recognitions that occur during psychosis is a strange notion, but for those who have actually experienced psychosis, we frequently come to understand that some of the ideas we developed during psychosis have a solid basis in our personal world. Sorting the static from the insights is central to regaining a more accurate perception of our world and strengthening our recovery. It is also essential in coming to grips with the double binds, contradictions, and trauma that lie at the heart of many of our experiences and to resolving these issues so we can move on with our lives.

The first step in counseling people in this phase is to allow us to talk about psychotic experiences and what meaning these experiences had for us. We often have ideas about the relationship between our personal life and the delusions and hallucinations that we had during psychosis. We often lack clarity about where consensus reality ended and our imaginations began. We also often need help in connecting the voices and contradictions of the people around us and our feelings, and real and imagined experiences during psychosis. We often lack understanding of how our personal life history created our very personal, symbolic experiences during psychosis and will tend to universalize our unique experiences. Even so, seeing post-psychotic schizophrenia as a potential treasure-trove of self-understanding and insight into our experiences will greatly help the counselor in aiding the person in therapy.

After there is a free discussion of the experiences and ideas during psychosis, attempts can be made to sort actual experiences from hallucinatory ones. Determining what experiences and perceptions can be verified through contact with other people who were present during the episodes or through talking to others about the person's life can help a person understand what was real and what was imagined. The focus should not be on whether or not these experiences can be fully verified but on what they mean to the person and his or her life history.

The next step is to link perceptions with real personal history and to identify the meaning of these perceptions. It is important to remember that delusions are often poetic expressions about how people feel about their lives. The ideas should be examined for their emotional content and what that says about the inner self. Actual events from the past may be found to be the basis of many delusions and obsessions during psychosis. Connecting the reality with the psychosis is very helpful in reintegrating people back into reality. It also strengthens the mental health by helping us come to grips with the real meanings of our psychotic experiences.

Revealing Secrets and Trauma

Oftentimes the core issues will involve long-held secrets and trauma that the person has found unbearable to endure. Coming to have some resolution of these secrets and the impact they have had on the person is often the key to restoring the individual to a normal, if medicated, state of mental health. The secrets and trauma may involve issues that cannot be resolved in the family, the community, or the world, and thus will require that the person resolve these issues through acceptance of difficult situations. The key is to help the person find ways to not be controlled or victimized by the situations that were hidden, ignored, or not healed previously.

Dealing with the secrets and trauma often places the counselor in a double bind. Frequently, problems within the family or community are revealed concerning the same people who may have heroically saved the client's life during his or her psychosis. Furthermore, the problems within a family or community may not be perceived as a difficulty by them, but they can be the source of deep contradiction and inner conflict for the person. In some troubled families or communities, the recovering person will become a scapegoat and the diagnosis is equated with being a permanent troublemaker. In these situations, the requirement that the person with schizophrenia live in a positive, emotionally healthy environment will be interpreted as a burden for people who are "content in their misery." On the other hand, for families and others who are willing to grow, the recovery can mean a parallel rebirth into a healthier, more life-loving way of living. In either case, for the person to heal, revealing the secrets and trauma of his or her life needs to be the first step in developing independence from inner and outer turmoil.

In some cases, such as when schizophrenia seems related to extreme trauma or ongoing conflict in the family or community, it is important that people with schizophrenia develop rules and practices which protect themselves from any further hardship. This may involve separating from those who are abusive or in some way toxic and developing a supportive groups of friends and counselors to strengthen their new resolve. This is especially important because contact with people, places and things that caused trauma often increases the symptoms of schizophrenia and can make rebuilding the person's life more difficult.

Regardless of the sources, the secrets and trauma are core issues that need to be healed before full recovery can be attained. In part, this healing will involve connecting the secrets, trauma, and real life history to the experiences during psychosis, and in part this healing will come from creating a new life that deals with these problems in a healthy and realistic way.

Facing Character Flaws and Resolving Inner Conflict

People with schizophrenia, like everyone else, often have one or more severe character flaws. Unlike some people, people with schizophrenia often experience distress and conflict because of these character flaws, especially during psychosis. Just as people with schizophrenia are more sensitive to turmoil and trouble than others, inner conflict and contradictions caused by character flaws may disturb the person with schizophrenia more than other people. At the same time, the problems of psychosis and chemical imbalance may make the character flaws in people with schizophrenia more exaggerated and difficult to deal with. In both cases, just as secrets and trauma need to come to the surface to be healed, the failings of people with schizophrenia must come into plain view and be successfully resolved. Unlike some people, most people with schizophrenia cannot negotiate life well if we have inner conflict about our character.

In dealing with character flaws in people with schizophrenia, it is helpful to link secrets, trauma, and character flaws with the distress, perceptions, and behavior during psychosis. In some cases, the behavior will be linked to attempts to find magical solutions to real and imagined failings. In other cases, feelings of guilt or persecution will give rise to self-destructive or paranoid behavior that has origins in the personal failings that people perceive in themselves. By linking the inner distress and problems with the psychotic symptoms, people with schizophrenia can see that they were working to resolve these conflicts in their own ways, even during psychosis.

The second step in dealing with character flaws in people with schizophrenia is to find the relationship between trauma, poor guidance, and other problems in childhood with the character flaws that developed in the individual. Seeing these character flaws as being part of the core problem that became exaggerated and overwhelming during psychosis helps make the process of recovery also one of spiritual renewal.

Once the difficulties bothering the person have been fully revealed and the life history has been established that tells the story of the inner life, the counselor and the person with schizophrenia need to set up an agenda for resolving the issues. Coming to terms with real and perceived inner problems also means resolving these issues so that the person's double binds and inner contradictions are successfully resolved.

Religious Conversions and Rigidity

It is fairly common for people with schizophrenia and other mentally ill people to undergo religious conversions during and after psychosis. These religious conversions are often marked by rigidity in beliefs and a tendency to want those around them to convert to the same thinking. The rigidity may also be connected to rituals and other behaviors that the mentally ill person insists on doing with a commitment that may seem to be obsessive. These religious conversions can be distressing to family members and others, who fear the religious conversion will lead to further difficulties.

In understanding the religious conversion, it is important to recognize that mentally ill people frequently lack willpower and exhibit numerous addictions, behavioral problems and character flaws. These problems are frequently as severe as the mental illness itself, such as extremes of substance abuse and acting out in anger, sexuality, and other dangerous behaviors. The mentally ill person is often aware of these problems and wishes to change, but lacks the willpower to achieve this goal. Successful religious conversions will result in near-miraculous change in these behaviors, suddenly and potentially permanently giving the person the strength to end negative behaviors and addictions. These behaviors are replaced by highly religious thinking, frequent rituals and reading of religious and spiritual texts, and changing social groups to match the new identity. These changes will appear to the mentally ill person as essentially proving the reality of their religion.

Despite the rigidity associated with religious conversions, the religious conversion is a process by which the mentally ill person is metaphorically expressing their new identity and often helps the person develop the willpower to become relatively functional in society. In spite of the rigidity of the conversion and the tendency to pick non-mainstream religions and spiritual practices, as long as the religion doesn't advocate self-abuse or violence or extreme bigotry against other groups, the change is often one for the better. People around mentally ill people should be careful that others in the religion don't take advantage of their vulnerability and dominate or control them in a cult-like way, but overall the approach should be similar to when working with a person in psychosis. First, one should seek to see the good seed in the problem by examining how the changes in behavior help the mentally ill person deal with addictions, secrets, and character flaws. Second, one should see discussions as situations where one is negotiating with the mentally ill person about what beliefs he or she will keep in the long term.

While the initial conversion is marked by rigidity in belief and behavior, as the person with schizophrenia becomes more assured of his or her new identity and lifestyle, he or she will become flexible and easy-going. After six months or a year has passed, those around the person can begin the process of seeking compromises that make the behavior less demanding on the person and family members and friends. In the meanwhile, numerous positive behaviors will be exhibited by the mentally ill person.

It is important to understand that while the changes can be extremely helpful, they do not replace counseling or healing of trauma. The behavioral changes associated with religious conversions rest on shaky ground as long as the trauma that underlies the addictions and character flaws goes unhealed. For that reason, counseling is still required for the post-psychotic person. Likewise, despite sometimes near-miraculous changes in addictive and negative behavior, medication is still normally necessary. Religious conversions that occur during psychosis are usually not long-lasting for that reason.

At the same time, it is also important to note that religious conversions can provide remarkably quick and helpful ends to addictive and anti-social behavior. In fact, in some cases, these conversions can actually provide faster and more solid changes in these behaviors than any present techniques used by counselors. For that reason, these changes should and must be respected as the mentally ill individual's personal solution to the double binds and negative behavior that underlie a person's delusions and fears. Even if the person with schizophrenia eventually stops following the religion, numerous positive behaviors and attitudes will often be retained from the values and beliefs of the religion.

Since the religious change is the individual's unique and symbolic response to personal trials and tribulations, religious conversion must originate with the mentally ill person. Religious people around the psychotic or post-psychotic individual may seek to convert the person to their religion, but in many cases this results in ineffective change at best because the conversion is happening prior to the person with schizophrenia having the necessary internal change and, more importantly, because the conversion doesn't express the unique solution to the person's double binds and trauma.

Attaining Inner Peace

For the person with schizophrenia, attaining inner peace is essential to maintaining a healthy and happy lifestyle. To do this, the person must resolve the secrets, trauma, and possible character flaws that make up the core of confusion which become highlighted and exaggerated during psychosis. Identifying real life history that created the basis for the person's inner conflict, connecting this history to the delusions and hallucinations experienced during psychosis, and resolving these problems in post-psychotic counseling will create meaning and strength from the process of schizophrenia.

Being forced by schizophrenia to face and deal with real life issues can make for a person who is stronger, mentally healthier, and more understanding of the human condition than someone who has never gone through counseling. By resolving trauma, secrets, and inner conflicts, the person can move past the ordinary problems that most people live with as a part of their normal lives and in place of those problems can attain inner peace and strength. This goal for counseling makes for a person who can return to mainstream society with a renewed sense of vigor and ability, with greater understanding, and with insight into the inner issues that affect many people, schizophrenic or not.

Putting into practice behavior that nourishes the person emotionally, such as regular times of relaxation and enjoyable habits, is part of attaining the necessary inner peace. As the person learns what things are upsetting and best avoided and what things are pleasant and helps strengthen his or her spirit, inner peace becomes more than a fixed idea. It becomes an ongoing condition where the person attains peace for an extended period of time and then maintains practices which nurture that peace during times of stress and problems.

To help with this process, the counselor should encourage the person with schizophrenia to set up regular practices that promote peace and calm and that provide enjoyment. Finding what is troubling to the person and working to lessen or eliminate those things from the individual's surroundings is helpful to maintaining a tranquil and calm environment. With the person's home as a peaceful base to move outward into the world, the person can meet more and more daily pressures with strength and fortitude. In doing so, the person develops the strength to live a predominantly normal life, ideally in the mainstream of society.

Attaining of a Healing Resolution

The work of Paris Williams in his Ph. D. thesis on people who have experienced psychosis provides substantial details on psychosis as part of a life journey. Seeing the psychotic experience as having a spiritual purpose akin to a hero's journey in allegorical myths, his work examines the journeys of six people who have been changed by their psychosis.

In looking at the case studies provided by the work, there appears to me to be different types of psychosis by theme and location of the experiences. For example, a man called Trent in the study experienced a messianic quest to save the whole of humanity; his theme was a heroic and messianic journey and the location of his beliefs was all of humanity and the whole world. In another case, a woman called Cheryl experienced the theme of extreme self-loathing, especially centered on her lack of worth as a partner and family member. In third example, a man called Byron experienced a heroic journey, but the location of his experiences was on spiritual realms, making his psychosis like to a visionary process.

In these cases, it is helpful to think of these experiences as expressing unanswered needs deep within the person. The different themes and locations of psychosis can provide clues about real-life changes that can bring about healing resolutions to these unanswered needs. In the case of people who are experiencing self-loathing, finding a means by which they can radically alter their self-perception to experience feeling fully loved by others can greatly alleviate their inner turmoil, as occurred in Cheryl's life. In the case of visionary experiences, finding a religious tradition or spiritual path that gives meaning and substance to these visions allows the person to place them into a coherent and structured set of practices, as Byron accomplished after many years of searching. In my own experience, applying the meaning derived from my psychosis (which contained both messianic and self-loathing aspects) into concrete changes in my daily life allowed a healing resolution that not only provided stability, but a happy and fulfilling life embedded in my family and community.

Having people tell our stories through psychosis contains the potential that a range of themes and locations of experiences can be identified and concrete and meaningful healing resolutions based on the unanswered needs can be identified. In this way, early in identifying a person's psychosis we could begin to develop a general plan to resolve underlying issues and move the person toward a much fuller, happier, and healthier life. Movement toward this resolution could possibly begin during psychosis itself and aid in calming the person and allying with his or her rational

core by showing that others are working to resolve these core inner needs. In this way, it may
be possible to provide powerful behavioral pre-
scriptions for positive changes based on the individual content of a person's psychosis.

Developing a New Identity

The process of life review during counseling is
aimed at the reintegration's thinking into a solid,
self-knowing, confident, and peaceful self. During
counseling it is important to understand that the
delusions and hallucinations experienced during
psychosis oftentimes were more than mere random ideas and events. They were the seeds of a
new personality and identity for the person with
schizophrenia, one which expressed the inner
turmoil, trauma, and secrets that hadn't been integrated into the personality prior to psychosis. In
the themes of the psychosis, the person with
schizophrenia poetically imagined transforming
their double binds and contradictions into a new,
happier reality.

The process of post-psychotic counseling
should have as a goal the gradual recognition of a
new identity, one that consciously recognizes the
inner experiences that remained hidden prior to
psychosis. By connecting the poetic delusions of
psychosis with the real life history and moving
the person toward resolving the inner and outer

conflicts that marked his or her life, the person with schizophrenia is aided in creating a new identity. This new identity should resolve the problems that troubled the person prior to and during psychosis. It should also serve as the basis for new directions in life, which will include ideas and insights which originated during psychosis.

As time passes and we make progress in resolving dilemmas and healing wounds, the directions of our lives should more and more take us out of ourselves and into a new life. As discussed in the following chapter, the counseling that people with schizophrenia undergo after psychosis should be paralleled by new directions in our personal and public life. We should move in expanding circles, first protected and relatively safe ones, and then increasingly into the more mainstream society. This movement should be the expansion of our new identity, taking new aspects of our self and our consciousness into account and providing solid ground for our new, healthy, and strong self.

EMDR and other Treatments for Trauma

Once counseling has reviewed our life experiences, connected them to our psychosis, and served as the basis for forming a new identity, we and our counselors will have a clear understanding of the sources of trauma in our lives-before, during, and after the psychosis. Liberating the person with schizophrenia from difficult inner conflict, suffering, compulsive behavior, and numerous other issues will be served by focusing on means to reduce the effect of the trauma on the person. By reducing the effect of long-standing trauma, it is possible to relieve the person of unwanted behavior and feelings that cause inner conflict and challenges.

While there are a number of therapeutic techniques which seek to reduce the effect of old trauma, the therapy that has worked for me is EMDR. Prior to use of the therapy, years of counseling had clearly identified the problems and trauma that were important factors in my life. Using this as a basis for the approach, the counselor and I outlined the main sources and events of trauma in my life history and began a slow, methodical process of going over individual incidents with EMDR to release me from their effect. The process proved very effective, allowing me to be freed from many old traumas and gave me a strong sense of inner peace and strength that I hadn't known at any time prior in my life.

While EMDR may not be effective for everyone, using this or similar treatments to heal emotional wounds and attain inner peace is a crucial final step in the development of a new person. Once the effect of old wounds is released, the person has learned the life lessons that the experiences had to teach without being limited by the emotional burden that accompanied them. Accordingly, the person with schizophrenia is liberated not only from old wounds but also graduates into a new sense of life and a new understanding of the meaning of his or her life.

Reviewing Mystical and Spiritual Observations

The final step in integrating the psychotic experience into the person with schizophrenia's life is to review the mystical and spiritual observations that occurred and glean their meaning. Learning that events like intuition and synchronicity are frequent parts of everyday life and can be trusted, albeit tentatively, for insight and understanding is helpful in making the person more understanding. Likewise, connecting mystical and spiritual observations during psychosis about human nature, the world as it exists, and one's own life is an important part of regaining respect for oneself as a person.

Many people with schizophrenia continue to see life through a mystical or spiritual lens after psychosis has ended. People with schizophrenia often consider larger issues of life, spirituality, religion, and meaning. Finding how these issues relate to our inner and personal lives, and learning to apply their lessons in our attempt to find inner peace and a new identity, is a crucial part of our complete recovery. Counselors should encourage thoughtful and insightful discussion of mystical, spiritual, and religious subjects while also encouraging these ideas to exist side by side with a practical and realistic lifestyle. In doing so, the spiritual renewal that so many people with schizophrenia attempt to gain through magical means during psychosis can be attained permanently and in our real life through counseling, reflection, and insight.

Spiritual Transformation

A significant finding from my review of ten essays completed by post-psychotic people is that most of them describe undergoing a spiritual journey during and after psychosis. Spiritual beliefs, practices, and group memberships were frequently different after psychosis than prior to psychosis. These changes were felt to be both welcomed by the person and perceived as allowing their inner nature as spiritual people to improve. These transformations were seen by the people as very positive steps that improved their ability to both express their inner nature and to live a life of their choosing. While these transformations were not always comfortable for the people around them, in the cases I know of the changes were generally recognized as aiding the people who have undergone the psychosis.

The purpose of this chapter is to aid in this spiritual transformation by outlining one means to move the person toward attaining it. From this perspective, recovery and transformation are seen as complementary processes of equal importance. Full recovery is difficult unless the seeds of change contained in the psychotic experience are given an environment in which they can grow. Transformation is likewise aided by a life in which the person can function effectively in the outside world. In this way, recovery and transformation are twin horses that can pull the person from a difficult situation into a full and deeply rewarding life.

Having the attitude that the person is unique and needs to be given respect is essential: for some, psychosis may have been a gift of insight that occurred side-by-side with confusion; others may find it to be an expression of what they did not want their life to be; and others may see it as only random events that serve no purpose. All these views may fit for different individuals in post-psychosis. Likewise, some may seek to fully suppress symptoms and not explore any form of personal growth or spirituality arising from the psychosis; others may gingerly explore their experiences and find meaning that they apply to their post-psychotic life; yet others may find means to live with what are considered symptoms of psychosis and seek to develop shamanic or similar mystical lifestyles. All of these are valid approaches to the varied nature of this experience so long as the person remains able to function and attain a life of their choosing.

Probably the best approach is to consider schizophrenia as an open-ended journey with many different possible destinations. All of the possible destinations above are healthy resolutions of the crisis we call psychosis and the choice of which of these paths (or some other) are taken is best chosen by the person who has experienced the crisis. Our role is to attempt to provide them with a safe passage to their destination.

CHAPTER SIX
REJOINING SOCIETY

At the same time that the person with schizophrenia is undergoing post-psychotic counseling, it is important to encourage the individual to begin the long process of rejoining mainstream society. This can be a very difficult for the person with schizophrenia, whose experience with trauma during psychosis and feelings of worthlessness and stigma can make contact outside of very narrow safe places frightening.

Due to the chaos of schizophrenic thinking, people with schizophrenia have feelings and perceptions that are much more instinctive than normal. In early recovery, people will continue to respond to situations with these very intense feelings. During initial contacts with other people after psychosis, people with schizophrenia tend to be very vulnerable to too much excitement or strong feelings and respond by fleeing the situation. This should not be cause for too much concern, as it is a means by which the person avoids a reoccurrence of symptoms because of stress.

In looking for ways to increase social activity for people with schizophrenia, it is important to think of people with schizophrenia as being very territorial. In some places or with some people, people with schizophrenia will feel safe and calm. Going into new places, encountering too many new people, or too much noise or intensity of feelings will frighten people with schizophrenia and force them to leave. As time passes and people with schizophrenia expand their territory, they will be able to deal with more people, places, and events. Thinking of the first few months and years of post-psychosis as expanding, step by step, their territories is helpful in creating the patience and understanding that is required for rejoining society.

Attending functions for the mentally ill, such as picnics, holiday events, and group therapy, are a way that people with schizophrenia can socialize in a safe environment. In some cases, people with schizophrenia will avoid other mentally ill people, often out of shame of the disease. Having family members go to some of the functions can be helpful in encouraging the person with schizophrenia to attend. In other cases, people with schizophrenia will cling to hanging out only with other mentally ill people, out of fear of the outside world. Using other means of expanding territory can help expand the social circle.

In many circumstances, the easiest means of expanding territory is to involve the person in family functions. Family members who have helped the person with schizophrenia will usually be appreciated and will be looked at as people who are safe. Having the person come to family functions, such as small reunions, and taking walks, going on picnics, and having simple family dinners can help expand the individual's territory. Having small groups of close friends and family visit the home every so often can help the person socialize with more people in a familiar place. In all of these situations, it is important to note how well or poorly the person responds to the visits and whom the person is comfortable with. Over time, the person with schizophrenia will be able to interact with more and more people comfortably. Encouraging a cautious step-by-step approach to this growth is helpful.

The person with schizophrenia may also have certain friends, homes, and hangouts that give comfort. These may be the homes of family friends or friends they have made over time, and may be hangouts like parks, bars and coffeehouses. People with schizophrenia can often attract friends who have various problems, as well as friends who are well-meaning and positive influences, and it is important to keep communication open about the people they hang out with, what they are doing, and how they are being treated. Like a lot of work with people with schizophrenia, it is helpful to have the attitude that people must learn their own lessons and come to their own conclusions about whom to be with, though this can require patience. Keeping communication open about their experiences is the most important goal, since that is the means by which parents and counselors can intervene in case of serious trouble. Over time, people with schizophrenia will learn to discern who can be trusted and who can't.

Another source of possible expansion is into church functions, since this is normally a relatively structured and safe environment. It is important to note the person's feelings and reactions to the church, and to avoid discussions of negative aspects of theology, such as hell, sin, and judgment. People with schizophrenia will remain emotional sponges for the rest of their lives and negative emotions arising from theology can be especially difficult. Negative religious beliefs can also be a source of obsession and fear, so this also needs watching. With these cautions, church functions can serve as safe places where people with schizophrenia can expand their base and meet sympathetic people.

Attending structured functions, such as public events like theater, musical events, movies, and similar happenings, is also a safe way for people to expand their sense of safe space. Structured events are easy to understand and have simple rules about behavior that can be understood and followed. In these events people don't have to worry about becoming someone's center of attention, so that allows them to relax in a crowd of people.

Over time, people with schizophrenia will gradually grow out of the shock of psychosis and come to accept themselves as they are. As this happens, their sense of safe territory and self-confidence will grow. Following a slow expansion of their social interactions can help them move forward into more and more mainstream events. They will also learn to recognize people who accept them and mean well toward them, making new friends and expanding their social circle.

Volunteering in Areas of Interest and Covenant of Good Works

Another means of expanding social contact is to volunteer with groups that reflect a person's area of interests. Prior to and during psychosis, the person with schizophrenia will often express concern about community and world problems, such as poverty, human rights, ecology, and war. Using this interest as a basis for encouraging a person to volunteer with like-minded and well-meaning groups can help the person grow in a number of ways.

In part, this process is one of developing a new identity, one that is in line with the consciousness he or she is developing in the counseling that parallels this growth. By making specific efforts to develop an identity in the real world, the person with schizophrenia meets like-minded people and expands his or her sense of self. By volunteering to work on projects that are aimed at improving the state of humanity and the world, the person makes positive contributions to the world and gains self-respect. The person can also make new friends and develop a wider social circle.

It is important that the groups that the person with schizophrenia volunteers with actually does acts of good works, such as feeding the hungry, providing housing for the homeless, reforesting or cleaning ecologically damaged areas, and so forth. My experience is that there exists what I call the Covenant of Good Works, wherein doing good works results in the reward of better situations in one's life. By taking part in good works, people can help move their life forward. Regardless of the idealism of the covenant, simply being in groups of people who are volunteering to improve the lot of humanity and the Earth places the individual with people who are generally kinder, more generous of spirit, and more willing to accept others without undue criticism or judgment. And, since the person with schizophrenia is helping them with a good cause, the people in the group are grateful that the individual is making the extra effort despite his or her own problems.

Retraining for New Work

As people with schizophrenia regain their bearings and expand their social circle, it is possible and often wise for them to consider retraining for work. This can be a frightening process due to complications involving health insurance and disability, and it is important that people with schizophrenia approach the process of renewed work with careful planning and fallback preparations should money or difficulties force them to return to some assistance.

There are two notable sources of work that often fit the needs and talents of people with schizophrenia. One is to retrain into some counselor position. As briefly noted earlier, a post-psychotic person who has come to some understanding of his or her psychosis can make an excellent mentor in a treatment team and will be in a position to be a good counselor in the post-psychotic phase of treatment. In some ways, this is the best use of the experience people with schizophrenia have, and makes for the possibility of an expanding comprehension of schizophrenia based on the work of those who understand the illness from all aspects.

A second source of possible work for people with schizophrenia is retraining for a career at an entry level position that has the possibility of rapid increases in salary, such as technical or engineering work. This work is possible for many people with schizophrenia because we often have technical or mathematical ability, despite the difficulties our brains have in other ways. Seeking to gain a technical degree or certificate can help move the person with schizophrenia into a place of being able to get a job and rejoining the mainstream workforce.

There are numerous other possible sources of work for people with schizophrenia, provided that insurance can be provided or afforded by the work. In seeking work, it is important that we compromise whatever preferences we have with what is feasible given that we have a major illness that requires ongoing medication. For the many people with schizophrenia who would like to pursue a career that cannot provide insurance, it is important to keep in mind that it may be possible to pursue their desires, such as art or writing, as a hobby while their work allows them to have a mainly normal life.

Interacting in Mainstream Society

After the person with schizophrenia has worked through initial stages of rejoining society, he or she will be able to interact with mainstream society with increasing frequency. I personally believe that this interaction is very important to growth and healing. By interacting in the mainstream, the person redevelops confidence and gets a wider perspective of how people think, feel, and act in the world. The person will be challenged to deal with the complexities of people outside the community of mentally ill people and their families, and will face both hardships and breakthroughs in dealing with others.

It is helpful for the person with schizophrenia to regularly reflect on people they meet with counselors, friends, family, and in personal journals. The person should look at this expansion into mainstream society as an exploration into the various personalities and quirks of human nature around him or her. Ideally, the person will come to have insights and perspectives on people that are deeper and more useful than those held by ordinary people. Once the person finds a way to understand the variety of normal people and the many different perspectives, beliefs, and personalities in the world around them, the person will be able to be comfortable with others. The person will probably discover that while most people don't need medication for chemical imbalances in their brains, most people do have quirks, character flaws, personal traumas, secrets, and hardships, just like people with schizophrenia, our families, our communities, and our world. Coming to accept the deep imperfections and contrasting strengths found in many people is often central to our recovery.

In interacting with mainstream society, mentally ill people face the choice of whether or not to be public about having our diseases. This choice should be made for deeply personal reasons, based on what the individual believes is best for their own mental health. My early childhood gave me a certain cantankerous nature that eagerly rejects unjustified stigma, and this blessed me with the ability to tell people from the earliest point in my recovery that I was a person with schizophrenia and I was proud to be one. As a person with schizophrenia, I am more sensitive, thoughtful, and conscientious than many ordinary people. I have endured more in my life than most people in industrialized countries ever have to suffer, and I cope with an illness that most people would not wish to face in their worst nightmare. The process of psychosis and recovery has given me insight into my life and spirituality, and I am a profoundly better person for having had schizophrenia.

As a person with schizophrenia who is out about being schizophrenic, I have found that people in mainstream society are more accepting of a normal-appearing person with schizophrenia than one might suppose. Most people who have prejudice about the mentally ill are frightened of us. Being public about our illness scares away those people and leaves only good-hearted and well-meaning people around us. One cannot expect much extra sympathy from mainstream people toward the mentally ill. As one discovers, mainstream people have their own problems, their own failings, and their own diseases, and as such are typically too involved with personal hardship and denial to spare energy toward others. Those people who do show sincere sympathy for the mentally ill are unusual people, as imperfect as any other, but often kinder and more understanding.

Choosing to be public about schizophrenia should not apply to one special area of life, and that is the job interview. Very few employers will take a chance on someone who tells them they have mental illness, and doing so is a virtual guarantee of being rejected. Once accepted for work and after any trial period, being public at the jobsite is usually helpful, since it creates an atmosphere where the person can feel safe to discuss the illness as daily events bring it into focus.

If the person feels that they do not wish to be public about their mental illness with mainstream people, however, that is the best course for him or her. In my case, being public has worked very well for me, but that is in large part because I have a personality that fits with that decision.

Having Positive Expectations

One of the most important things that people with schizophrenia learn to do in early recovery is to allow other people to define our reality. One of the most important things that other people can do is to have positive expectations. As people redevelop a sense of self, the attitudes of family, friends, and counselors will define our perceived limits and the sort of life we expect to have. Beginning with gradual steps into greater and greater autonomy, having confidence in the person to one day have a life as fully functioning as any other ordinary person is crucial to giving a person the confidence to succeed. The family will have to balance confidence with observations of what the person can do at the stage of recovery he or she is in at that time, but having the belief that the person can one day fully recover can be crucial in that happening.

As is evident from the remote controls that lie about people's houses and pizzas that are delivered to our doorsteps, the tendency for most people to be lazy when given the opportunity is widespread. While it is true during psychosis and early recovery that pushing a person to do something is often counterproductive, once recovery has been established and stabilized, it is important that the person be encouraged to do chores, to have good hygiene, and to once again fit into the normal standards of family and social behavior. The trauma and overwhelming nature of psychosis is not permanent, and once the person begins to recover and grow as a person, expectations create the basis for how the person defines him or herself and the chances to have a normal life. Saying that we are condemned to half a life because we have schizophrenia is as counterproductive as saying we should have a normal life during psychosis. Give us the encouragement to try to have a normal life, and if we fail, at least we've had the opportunity to try.

Finding Trusted Individuals to Define Reality

The final and permanent component of recovery for people with schizophrenia is to continue to find trusted individuals to define reality for us. As we grow and expand in post-psychosis, we will gain more and more people whom we trust and can rely on for help in understanding the world. As we continue to grow out into the world, we will need to find people in the various settings that we are in to help confirm with us our perceptions and insights.

As time goes on, we will gain more and more ability to make judgments about reality on our own. However, making close connections with people and being able to share our perspectives is essential to full recovery. Once we leave the family home, it is important to find one or more people with whom we can share our daily life and reflect on the accuracy of our perceptions. Ideally, that will be in the form of a partner with whom we will share our daily life. Given the one requirement of someone to act as a sounding board, the person with schizophrenia in full recovery can lead a mainly normal life.

AFTERWORD

The aim of this purposefully short book is to provide a blueprint for recovery from schizophrenia. It is based on the experience I have as a person with schizophrenia gifted with a fortunate life, and my experience in helping other people with schizophrenia through psychosis and post-psychosis. I see it as one in what will hopefully someday be a number of blueprints for recovery written by people with schizophrenia.

I sincerely believe that there are different forms of schizophrenia and different therapies that are successful with these different forms. This blueprint only reflects the forms of schizophrenia I have encountered and what has worked in these situations. I encourage the reader to actively discern what steps seem to work with individual people with schizophrenia and apply this blueprint according to what works in each individual case. Ultimately, like intuitive ideas of what the future may hold, the proof of what treatment works for any given person is in how things turn out.

May your life turn out well for you.

APPENDIX A
HOW A SERIES OF
HALLUCINATIONS DEVELOPS A
STORY

Hallucinations often occur in a series of related episodes that build a story and gain intensity and depth of meaning as they go on. Hallucinations seem to reveal a hidden reality and, because they are mixed with intuitive experiences and personal information similar to dreams, create a stepwise building of delusional frameworks within the psychotic individual. Hallucinations are often highly personal and symbolic experiences that are taken by the person with schizophrenia as real experiences with universal implications and literal meanings. The series of three hallucinations summarized below occurred over a period of about six weeks in the mid-to-late summer of 1985, resulting in extreme psychosis and a highly agitated state. These hallucinations occurred after two and a half years of psychosis and had been preceded by years of similar hallucinations and delusions.

In the first hallucination, which lasted less than a minute, I was walking toward the doors of a bus station with a small lunch when I looked through the glass doors and saw a street person looking at me. The street person's eyes were highly unusual—they seemed more like landscapes that went back into the man's head infinitely far, stretching on for eternity. I thought to myself, "That man has eyes like God." I walked through the bus station doors and the man asked me if I had a cigarette. I said no and sat down to eat my snack. The man wandered off and another man strolled by, laughed, and said, "You must be waiting for someone." He then walked off. An hour or two after I left the station on the bus I concluded that the man had been God, and was waiting for me to offer him some of my food as an act of charity and good will. I supposed that God would have then offered me help with the problems I was facing.

The second hallucination occurred two weeks later when I was hitchhiking back to the town where I went to college in a state of agitation. The trip back, which took a day and a half, was filled with minor hallucinations and odd experiences. Reality seemed in flux around me and I decided that I would try to find Jesus to help me. I began to talk in code to my rides, hoping that Jesus would respond to my coded prayers. As I got into a pickup truck with a man with shoulder-length hair I saw that his eyes were similar to the man's eyes I had seen a couple weeks earlier. They didn't stretched back into his head as far, but had a depth that seemed to imply an ancient spirit. The man used a play on the words of my coded prayer, indicating that he was Jesus. In the next few minutes I had a brief conversation with Jesus, during which he pardoned my sins and told me that I could go to heaven if I now choose to follow God's path for me. He then told me to go into the woods and starve myself to death as penance and I would go to heaven. After he dropped me off, I went into the woods by the road for a short time, but decided to stay on Earth and do good works. As I returned to the road, I heard a voice say, "This means I will carry your cross" and my right forefinger touched my left wrist, as if marking where a nail would go in. I thought I was receiving a message teaching me sign language.

A couple weeks after returning, I attended a meeting of a self-help group. During the meeting another member and I went into another room to discuss how to approach counseling others. The other person with schizophrenia touched her right forefinger to her left wrist and looked at me, making me think that I was about to be crucified in some way and she was offering to help me with my trial. We returned to the meeting and after a few minutes events become very personal and powerful. The self-help group turned its attention entirely to the leader and me, and we had a long dialogue about my personal problems. The person I had met with privately fell silent, but her eyes became extremely pained and glazed over, as if foreseeing tremendous suffering. From the conversation that I had with the group leader, I came to believe that I was to be punished for disobeying God and Jesus and not fulfilling my penance. I left the meeting in an agitated state and began to believe that I was in jeopardy of going to hell. After spending the next twelve months believing that I had actually been condemned to hell with no chance of repentance, I called the group leader and another member of the self-help group and described what I had experienced. As it turned out, I had actually had a twenty to thirty minute hallucination that had begun when I met privately with the group member and lasted until the end of the meeting. I haven't any clear knowledge of what happened after the hallucination began, how long the meeting lasted after that moment, or anything else connected to consensus reality. All I know for sure was the twenty to thirty minute memory was a symbolic message which I misinterpreted as actual reality.

APPENDIX B
NOTES ON COMMON ELEMENTS
WITHIN DELUSIONS

This is a summary of notes from a schizo-phrenic research group that I participated in with three other men in post-psychosis. The intent was to outline common elements of our experiences during psychosis. Though we were only able to meet a few times, substantial progress was made in finding elements common to most or all of our experiences.

Prior to the group meeting, I had noted at least three general scenarios for psychotic delu-sions: Some people imagine themselves as arche-types of religious nature; others imagine them-selves as movie stars or other cultural icons; and a third group imagines scenarios involving aliens influencing events on Earth. While these three scenarios may blend into each other, I noted that in the post-psychotic review group that all four of us had experiences following the first scenario—we all imagined highly religious events with our-selves as major spiritual entities (One imagined that he was Jesus, the other three believed that they were the Devil or the Antichrist). Since the participants were all white males with some form of college education living in Midwest, this and other similarities may reflect a cultural bias.

Our group agreed that schizophrenic delusions contain a grain of truth. We noted the following ways that this had taken form in our experiences:

(1) As a general truth that is expressed metaphorically — an example of this is the historical aphorism that "To the victor goes the spoils" being expressed in a belief that killers are rewarded with wealth and status and combined with the delusional interpretation that people around the person in psychosis would announce their willingness to kill for wealth and status by saying the two words "I am".

(2) As a truth in one's personal reality expressed metaphorically — an example of this being a delusion of an intense, universal struggle between good and evil that was paralleled by the person in psychosis having positive and negative choices in his life.

(3) Accurate intuitions that appear in hallucinations.

(4) Coincidental events that lead to the idea that a mystical world is a reality underlying daily life.

(5) Many negative delusions originating from stress.

(6) Delusions having origins in experiences of the schizophrenic, some real and some hallucinatory.

(7) Delusions reflected by people who believe some version of the delusion, such as ordinary people having a belief in aliens, impending Rapture or other horrific ends of the world, or in people having psychic abilities.

(8) Stress triggering hallucinations and delusional thoughts.

In addition to these sources of delusional beliefs from real life experiences, three or four of us shared most of the following elements of the common world view below.

(1) Belief in an immediate danger of an apocalyptic end of the world.

(2) Control of most people into being blind to this reality by a nefarious, subliminal medium, including some combination of TV and/or radio, magic or mind control, "staging" of reality and a hidden conspiracy underlying the control.

(3) Division of the world into black-and-white good people verses bad people, with bad people including anyone trying to stop the quest for personal and world salvation discussed below.

(4) An ongoing battle of good against evil, centered on us.

(5) The person coming to believe that he is the apex of good or evil in one's culture (one person believed that he was Jesus/God and the other three believed they were the Anti-Christ/Devil).

(6) Extreme forms of mysticism, including belief in mind-reading being common, signs, oracles and a very dynamic reality where miracles and magic change fate through mind over matter.

(7) Multiple potential realities that we might may shift into at any moment, including the possibility of heaven or hell suddenly occurring for the whole world through magic, ritual, prayer or other powerful and miraculous event.

(8) Fascination with words and the belief that words contain hidden meanings, followed by a quest to uncover the underlying meanings and symbols of words that was part of a larger quest to uncover the magical means to save oneself and the world.

(9) Making up words to express new beliefs and experiences.

(10) Original ideas that are foreign to our own backgrounds but are found in the cultures of other people, including that human souls can be reborn as animals if they are sinful in their human incarnation and plants have a consciousness of their own.

(11) Explanation of symptoms, such as hearing voices or having psychosomatic pain, within the framework of the delusional world view. For example, we believed voices we heard were thoughts of other people or spirits that we were surrounded by.

(12) A focus on death, especially in a transcendent sense. The death could be of ourselves or the death of a loved one and could be combined with the belief that we should die, that someone else wants us to die, or that one has died and been reborn.

Our belief that mind reading was common can illustrate some of the details of these delusional ideas. In this example, we believed that some sort of mind reading was contained in a hidden aspect of computers or television and feared that others would hear our private thoughts. One person would selectively go mute around certain people in an attempt to prevent the mind reading; another found that his mind would internally scream obscenities when he thought his mind was being read. One person referred to uninvited mind-reading as "trespassing" and thought it was connected to the prayer that contains "And forgive our trespasses, as we forgive those who trespass against us."

The origin of the belief in mind reading included in one case hearing people's voices around their heads even though they weren't speaking and having an accurate intuition about what a person was about to do based on a voice. Another person heard the voice of his late Grandmother around the time of the first anniversary of her death. This experience, combined with a series of thoughts and other experiences caused him to believe that the CIA was seeking to control people's thoughts.

In looking for outside support of this idea, we noted that the media has numerous examples of ads for people who are "psychic". This had given us the impression that our experiences with hearing voices were not unique, but rather were being experienced by others as well.

APPENDIX C
INFORMAL SURVEYS OF
EXPERIENCES OF PSYCHOSIS

During 2011 I undertook a pilot study in which I asked ten self-identified post-psychotic people to answer several questions about their experiences. While the answers were open-ended and many questions were only partially answered, substantial insight into common experiences of people in psychosis seems possible from these essays. I review the questions and summarize the responses below.

(1) Did any of your psychotic experiences contain a grain of truth? For example, did you have experiences that in some way were intuitively accurate, that gave insight into real life, that seemed to symbolize something, or that were odd or coincidental experiences? Did the experiences support your delusional beliefs?

Seven of the ten respondents said that their experiences did contain some real elements; of the three that said no, one person only described a single incident in their response and another experienced only brief intervals of psychosis followed by interventions by a loving and trusted spouse. Given this, it appears to me that most people who have extended periods of psychosis find elements of truth within them.

Specifically, four people identify accurate intuitions during their psychosis, including a hallucination seen while on horseback that caused a person to decide to return home shortly before a storm blew up and a premonition of a car accident by the person's wife. In another case, a person in psychosis was talking over the phone to a person who had been intending to diet and smelled chocolate when none was around. The person in psychosis asked the other person if they had been eating chocolate and the person admitted that they had.

In addition to these examples, two people reported that their psychosis contained insights of value to them, one indicating that he saw his journey through psychosis as containing "mythic" qualities that were metaphors he could apply to his life. The other person indicated that beliefs during psychosis contained wisdom that were ignored and devalued by the people around them. Two other people indicated that they also felt the psychosis contained metaphoric beliefs that they could apply to their own life. One person reported a series of coincidences that provided meaning and insight into their life and philosophy.

In addition to these responses, three people commented that their hallucinatory or delusional experiences paralleled their real life. For example, Biblical verses that were they had read seemed to manifest or be projected in their real lives within a few hours or days of reading the passages.

Given all of these responses, it seems that people in psychosis experience real life events that in some way support the delusional framework that builds during that time.

(2) In looking at the origin of your delusional beliefs, did you read, see in the media or the internet, or hear about ideas from others that developed into delusional beliefs? For example, did you read a book about spirituality, religion, philosophy, the supernatural, aliens, etc., that became the basis for delusional ideas? If so, please describe the source and how your beliefs developed.

In this case, seven people indicated that beliefs had arisen from media sources, with some people indicating that beliefs were also shared with people in their religious group. The most common source of delusions was the Bible, with three of the seven people indicating that it had been a source of misunderstanding and delusion. Six of the seven people identified books as being the basis for delusions and four of the seven indicated that television and/or radio had been sources.

(3) Did you have any hallucinations or delusions that seemed to be triggered by stress? If so, can you describe the stress and the experiences you had?

In this case, seven people identified stress as triggering hallucinations or delusions and the other three people either did not answer or provided unclear answers.

(4) During psychosis, did you see yourself as being on a magical or spiritual quest to achieve something great? If so, please describe the quest(s), explain the goal(s), and explain what led you to believe that the magical or spiritual quest was possible.

Again, seven people answered that they saw themselves as on a spiritual question, with two people indicating they did not feel that way and one person providing an unclear answer. The two people who indicated they did not see themselves on a spiritual quest either described a single incident or experienced psychosis only very briefly prior to being convinced that they were hallucinating. Given this, it appears that the belief in a magical, spiritual quest is a very common aspect of fully developed psychosis.

It is noteworthy that a number of the respondents indicated that they felt that the spiritual quest was continuing in post-psychosis, either transformed into working with changing the world around them or as part of a new spiritual identity.

(5) Did you make up special words or phrases or give special meaning to words based on your experiences? Did these words have special or magical power? Can you list these words and what they meant to you?

Six people reported either making up special words or giving words special meanings, whereas three people reported that they did not do this. The other answer was unclear. The Bible was one source of special meaning for words, but, generally speaking, the words and phrases that contained special meaning appear to be very idiosyncratic and not to necessarily form a pattern from one person to the next. From this it is clear that people in psychosis will frequently have special meanings for words and phrases, but attempting to find out what these meanings are will take special time, effort, and trust on the part of the people around them.

(6) What led you to realize that you were experiencing hallucinations and/or delusions?

While several people did not clearly answer this question, three reported normal medical sources, such as a book on schizophrenia or re-

peated hospitalizations, as helping them understand that they were in psychosis. Three others
indicated that a trusted person—a friend or close
family member—had been the key in their decision to accept diagnosis. Given this, there is reason to believe that building relationships of trust
between outsiders and people in psychosis can be
helpful in moving people into early recovery. These relationships of trust can be built on CBT,
LEAP, Open Dialogue, or the techniques advocated in this handbook.

APPENDIX D
RELATED WEBSITES

The following are websites that contain approaches or organizations that seek to help with psychosis. While they do not all share the same perspectives on treatment approaches, I include various websites to allow for as much diversity of options as possible.

Therapies

Listen-Empathize-Agree-Partner

http://leapinstitute.org/

CommonGround and Personal Medicine

http://www.patdeegan.com/

Cognitive Behavioral Therapy

http://www.nacbt.org/

Wellness Recovery Action Plan

http://www.mentalhealthrecovery.com/

Schizophrenia: A Blueprint for Recovery

http://www.schizophreniablueprint.com/

Best Practices in Schizophrenia Treatment

http://www.neomed.edu/academics/bestcenter

Online Crisis Intervention Techniques Library

http://www.neomed.edu/cjccoe/index.php/crisis_intervention_team/training-calendar

Organizations

National Alliance on Mental Illness

http://www.nami.org/

Mental Health America

http://www.nmha.org/

National Mental Health Consumers Self-Help Clearinghouse

http://mhselfhelp.org/

National Empowerment Center

http://www.power2u.org/index.html

National Coalition for Mental Health Recovery

http://www.ncmhr.org/

Recover Resources

http://www.recoverresources.com/index.html/

National Association of Peer Specialists

http://www.naops.org/

Schizophrenics Anonymous

http://www.sardaa.org/

Information

Schizophrenia Magazine

http://www.mentalwellnesstoday.com/Schizop
hrenia.aspx

Schizophrenia Online Forum

http://www.schizophrenia.com/

APPENDIX E
MATERIALS SUPPORTING
MENTORING

This instruction sheet and essay are discussed in Chapter Two.

Instructions to the Understanding Mentor

The mentor and other members of the treatment team should read the essay before deciding to give it to the person in question. There should be agreement on the approach being advocated. Copies of the essay may be made for this purpose.

Ideally, this essay should be given to the person by the mentor as soon as possible after diagnosis and treatment has begun. It should be the only part of *Schizophrenia: A Blueprint for Recovery* given directly to the person until they are stable and (usually) on medication for at least a year. It should either be removed from the rest of the book or copied for this purpose.

The purpose of this essay is to begin a dialogue with the person in psychosis about their experiences. It is not intended to convince him or her to take medication. Rather, it is to help with the mentor/realist approach outlined in Chapter Two of *Schizophrenia: A Blueprint for Recovery*. If successful, the person with schizophrenia will begin to talk to the mentor and others about their experiences and their understanding of what has been happening during their psychosis.

For the purposes of getting the person to feel comfortable talking about this, their experiences are for the most part called a "vision quest" in the essay. This will provide a neutral terminology for the treatment team and the person to begin to discuss his or her experiences.

Follow the guidelines for the mentor in Chapter Two as the person with schizophrenia begins to talk about their experiences. Building and maintaining trust is paramount to calming the person and giving them someone to turn to during crises.

Ideally, the person with schizophrenia will begin to do reality checking, both on major incidents in the past, and in the present time, to confirm or deny their experiences. While many experiences will be found to be inaccurate, some seemingly improbable experiences, like the ones discussed in the essay, may turn out to have really occurred.

As the process of reality checking continues, the person with schizophrenia will eventually find that they cannot negotiate consensus reality while having hallucinations/visions. They will also find that some of their hallucinations are incorrect. By doing so, their rational core will come to understand that they need to take medication to live a happy, normal life.

As indicated above and in the accompanying book, this is seen as a long-term process where the trust and safety of the person with schizophrenia is placed above the desire for an immediate, short-term solution. However, by implementing these steps, the paranoia of the person will be reduced and the possibility of a more rapid recovery is increased.

Saving the World, Saving Yourself

This is written for people who are very concerned about saving the world. This may be the whole world, your personal world, people you love, saving yourself spiritually, or all of these. If you are like some people, you have been going through a personal and spiritual awakening that has given you insights and an understanding of things that is far different than what you perceived only a few years ago. These insights are both true for you in a very personal way and true for the world—indeed, the universe—at the same time.

If you think back to before you began to have these insights and experiences, you probably had a fairly mundane and "normal" consciousness about things. However, time and experience has opened new realms to you, new experiences that point simultaneously to something far better than what has been and, at the same time, portend the possibility of very hard times—even a cataclysm—for the world. And you, with your insights and perceptions, see the opportunity to help people avoid the negative and achieve the positive.

However, instead of your insights being recognized and your being able to help people, you have been diagnosed as having schizophrenia. People are saying, in essence, "You haven't seen what you've seen, take this pill and it will be all be better." If you think back to before you began to have the insights you've had, you can see that the experiences you had—mystical, spiritual, extraordinary, and so forth—might have seemed impossible to you then. Since you've had these experiences and gained these insights, you know that they are possible, and it can be very frustrating when people try to convince you otherwise.

I want to make clear at the outset that I have schizophrenia and have experienced hallucinations and delusions. I know that this doesn't mean that you have schizophrenia and have experienced what I have. However, I ask that you take time to read what follows and bear with me as I talk about things. I think I may have some helpful ideas that might be useful to most people, regardless of anything else.

At the very beginning of this, I can offer two pieces of advice that might be helpful. One is that you need to find someone to trust, someone who will not tell your secrets and insights to others, and confide in them. This will help you not feel all alone. The second one is that while you work on increasing your insights and preparing for the day when everything comes together, it will be helpful for you to look after yourself. In other words, to help others, you will need to survive until the miraculous event occurs that changes everything for the better. If you have someone to trust and confide in, you will be able to talk to them not only about your insights and experiences, but how you can survive while you wait for the big change.

I can't be sure of what you are experiencing, but I can offer some things that you might have experienced that are very important to you. You may have found out that it is possible to know what other people are thinking by hearing their thoughts. From this and other events you have realized that there is a universal spirit that connects us to each other, so you may be picking up thoughts of people that are very far away or in other dimensions or realities. You also may be very concerned about people reading your thoughts when you don't want them to.

Moreover, you may have realized that we are all connected spiritually, so when events seem to happen "by chance" they are not chance at all. They are, in fact, happening because of the connections between people.

You may have seen, or are in the presence of, very special beings. These may include a deity or angel who is very special to you, people or beings who are taking the form of being a guide to you, and possibly more negative beings. You may have realized that extraordinary beings are present with us on the Earth, and those who do not recognize this lack the insight that you have.

Likewise, you may have insights into the world's problems and the possibility of very positive or negative events in the near future. These events may take the form of something positive like Heaven coming onto Earth or something negative, like a terrible calamity brought on by war, ecological problems, starvation, pollution, and other things. These world problems may also have direct impact in your personal world and even within you. You are motivated to seek the positive—in the world as a whole, in your personal world, and within yourself. Yet many people around you are clearly blind or uncaring about these problems and the need for rapid change for the better.

This change for the better may be attainable through the mystical, spiritual, and otherwise extraordinary powers that you have been learning about in the last few years. Perhaps something miraculous can and will happen through an extraordinary event, and both the psychic connections you see around you and/or the extraordinary beings are helping bring this about.

These events may be going on inside of you, as well as outside of you. Your sensitivity to spiritual energy may have made you aware of changes in energy within you. You may have even had an experience of being imbued with the presence of an extraordinary being, hopefully something positive for you. Or you may sense a negative energy within you that you feel a need to cast out in some way. Obviously, these are important issues, and you would like to have friends to help you through this time.

Events may imply that people, extraordinary beings, or others are manipulating reality around you to move you toward a special fate or outcome. Perhaps people or beings are putting on a show for you, moving you towards your destiny, step by step, and those behind the scenes know what you will do and how all this will end.

Still, with all of these possibilities, people are clearly unaware of what you are experiencing. In general, people seem to be unconscious of what is going on. It is possible, even likely, that things like television and various organizations are controlling people's minds so that they can't see what you are seeing. It may be possible to somehow gain control of the means of controlling things like television and move people toward the miraculous change for the better.

From these experiences, you may have realized that you are in the center of multiple potential realities, some very positive, some very negative. Since your discovery of the extraordinary and psychic energies, beings, and events that can and have been occurring around you, you realize that even small events can lead to huge changes, possibly very quickly. You may have been aware of reality or consciousness shifts as they have happened and you may have noticed how few other people seem attuned to these changes. You may have, after a period of searching, discovered the plan or pattern of events that will lead to the big change that is coming. It may simply be a matter of time.

You may have also discovered that you, and others, have the ability to shape reality and the future by thoughts, words, rituals, and/or symbols. You know this because you have seen it work with your own eyes. You may have perceived that it is so common that sometimes the problem is not having psychic, magical, or miraculous events happen, but, instead, making sure that a casual thought, word, or action doesn't trigger something without you consciously intending for it to happen.

Many or all of these extraordinary things you have experienced in your own life and with your own senses, so you are certain of their existence. Since you have become open to seeing the reality that underlies mundane reality, you may have been in the presence of deities or angels or other extraordinary beings. You have seen intuition and possibly dreams become true in real life or shape reality around you. You may have had a sense for what was about to happen and it did occur. You have probably experimented with some form of mind over matter and found that you can shape the physical world with thought, word, or ritual. You may have also discovered psychic connections between people that linked seemingly chance events, showing you that you are well-founded in your beliefs. All of these things you have seen, so you are certain of them.

You have also, as said before, probably experienced times when reality seems to be in flux or to be shifting. Whether it's called a reality shift, a consciousness shift, or being taken to another place or time, you have experienced it and seen the effects clearly. Extraordinary travel through time or space may have occurred to you, and during this travel you gained knowledge that few people know. At the same time, you may have seen signs or portents of things to come.

You have learned, or are learning, that there are special or hidden meanings in words, letters, and sounds. Uncovering the pattern that underlies these symbols and meanings is important in liberating yourself and the world from the problems around it. You probably have devoted time and study to discovering these connections.

Through all of this there are also lesser psychic or extraordinary events, such as a passing voice that coincides with your thoughts, an occasional sound behind your head that doesn't have an earthly origin, or small colored lights appearing and disappearing in your normal vision. You are less sure of what these things mean, since they are passing and temporary, but they are more indications that there is a reality that underlies the reality around you.

In the midst of all these exciting discoveries and experiences you have become aware of a struggle between positive and negative forces, certainly outside of you and possibly within you as well. There is little doubt that the positive forces will win in the end, but your role in helping that happen is important. If you have an internal struggle that corresponds to the external one, you hope to be able to overcome the negative inside of you and in your life, and you seek people to help you on your quest for spiritual attainment. Again, you would like to have someone as a friend in this struggle, and, if you are lucky, you may have someone.

The key to all of these discoveries and struggles is the mystical or extraordinary solution that you have been seeking. Your experiences have directed you on a path that gives you hope that you can discover the plan or pattern that will allow you to rapidly manifest the best reality possible for as many people as possible. It is possible that you feel on the verge of this discovery, if you haven't made it already. Or, you may feel that you are in very serious spiritual trouble.

Obviously, these are very dramatic and important discoveries and events. As important as all of this is, I want to ask your patience as we discuss the mundane events around you and what people around you may be thinking about your experiences.

As you probably know, some people around you don't believe you've experienced these things. They believe that you have imagined all of this. They think the solution to all of these problems is to take a pill so you will stop having these experiences. As difficult and frustrating as it is, they are probably doing this out of concern for your health and well-being in an ordinary sense.

However, you know you are sane. You know what you've really experienced, and since they weren't with you when you experienced these things, they shouldn't tell you that they didn't happen. After all, they don't know these things didn't happen, they just don't believe in these things. And, as someone who is writing this and who doesn't know you, I can't tell you that you are imagining this. After all, how would I know?

You know you are sane because, as I said earlier, you're having accurate insights and intuition/psychic events. For example, you may have learned things about world, societal, family, or personal patterns that you didn't realize before. And, even though some people might not want to believe these things, you can see that they are true and important. In one example, a person might realize that emotional patterns in their family amount to abuse, or that society rewards some people for being violent or destructive. Not everyone wants to believe these things, but they are examples of things that you might have realized.

You may have also examples of accurate intuition or psychic events that happened in real life. For example, once I was talking to a guy and I left the room we were in. I decided I wanted to say something else to him and I turned around to go back in the room. But I heard his voice come through the door, saying, "Let me open the door." The wall between us was solid concrete and the door was solid and without any window, so I didn't have any visual or auditory cues to tell me what was about to happen. I paused, and a moment later the guy walked out of the room. I talked to him, said what I wanted to say, and left. From this I concluded that I was hearing people's thoughts.

There may also be examples of signs. For example, I one time saw a rainbow when I was returning from visiting friends I had just met. The rainbow was in the sky between me and the new friends, and I decided I could trust them. As time went by, I lost a lot of friends, but the people on the other side of the rainbow stood by me and were my best friends and confidants for ten years.

There may also be examples of visions or something like that which tell you accurate things. For example, once I was in a store with some other new friends. We were standing in a circle and for a moment reality swirled around us, so that only the three of us seemed lasting and real. I concluded that the three of us were all part of the same soul and we were deeply connected.

I left the town where I met these two friends and returned two years later. The town is a college town, and my friends weren't from there, so I didn't know if I would ever see them again. However, a few months after I returned, I happened to run into them walking down the street. We got to know each other and for the next year we were constant companions—they even happened to move in next door to where I was living. We became close during that year and reflected on our lives together. Eventually, I moved out of town for work, but knowing them for that year confirmed to me that my original vision two years earlier had been somehow accurate.

These are all examples of things that I've experienced that are true. You probably have some examples like that, too.

Despite this, people don't believe or understand what you are going through. If you think about it, a few years ago, you probably wouldn't have believed someone who told that you would go through what you already have. Thinking back to how you thought before these experiences, you might be able to understand why others have a hard time believing you. After all, you probably didn't believe most of these things were possible a few years ago. In the same way, the people around you who haven't experienced these things think the way you did only a few years ago.

The other reason that people think what they do about your experiences is that they match experiences of people like me who do have schizophrenia. In this short essay, I've described the reality that I knew when my brain chemistry changed and I went through an unrecognized and involuntary vision quest. It is true that I learned a lot from these experiences, and I am glad that I learned what I did. But through checking with other people I found that many things that I thought had happened really hadn't happened. They were symbolic visions that I mistook as literal events in physical reality.

I learned that I was on a vision quest, with seamless hallucinations that I couldn't separate from mundane reality, by reality checking. I talked to good people I trusted who were present at some of important events that occurred and I discovered that while they had occurred for me, they hadn't occurred for the other people. That is why it is important to find people you trust, so you can check what you experience with them and see if they experience what you do. If they do, then you and they share the same reality. If they don't, then you may want to consider ending the vision quest so you can have a safe, happy life.

If you have had extraordinary experiences with people you trust present, you might consider contacting these people and asking them about the experiences you had. Regardless of what you find out, doing this will probably help provide clarity to what happened.

People ask me what is the difference between a mystical point of view and what I experienced. What I always say is that the primary difference is that I was hallucinating—that is, on an involuntary and unrecognized vision quest—and that made it difficult for me to deal with everyday reality.

The other main difference is that people on vision quests tend to be even more mystical than mystical people. For example, a mystical person will tend to believe in a universal mind or spirit that connects people, but not in mind-reading or other conscious manifestations of the universal mind. This is because, as was true during my vision quest, that the experiences I had were symbolic but I took them literally, so I had a greatly exaggerated view of mystical thinking. This actually turned out to be a relief to me, because I discovered that the crisis I was in wasn't nearly as bad as I thought because the vision quest had exaggerated its severity.

I found that for my well-being and the well-being of the people I loved that I had to end the vision quest. This is because during the vision quest I had hallucinations and false memories that were seamless from ordinary reality, and so I misinterpreted symbolic events as real, physical events. Even with the accurate events I talked about earlier, there was so much misinterpretation of what happened that I couldn't function well.

This is in line with how vision quests are treated in cultures where they are recognized. Once the lessons of the vision quest have been given through the symbolic experiences, the vision quest is ended and the person rests and heals up from their experiences. This way, the lessons can be understood and applied to the person's life.

Obviously, I can't say that all this holds true for you. That is a decision for you to make. You might consider contacting people you trust to verify some of your experiences, or finding someone to trust to talk about all of your experiences. That will help you find friends and allies to make your own decision about these things.

While you consider possibly contacting people you trust who were present during your important experiences, or finding people who you can trust, I urge you to commit to loving yourself while events unfold. This means caring for yourself and treating yourself gently. If you are looking for a sign or a message on how you should proceed with life, I can offer this: You are loved by the Deity and the Deity wants you to live a long, happy life on this Earth. This is true for the person who gave you this essay, too. The person who gave you this essay deeply cares about you and wants you to live a long, happy life. They may not understand everything you are going through, but you might consider trusting them as much as you feel you can.

Regardless of the decisions you make about these things, I have some concrete suggestions that may help you with your situation. They are ways that you can seek to save yourself spiritually and physically, so you can be better able to make the positive changes you want to make.

Here's a list of things to consider doing for yourself and your loved ones.

— Treat your home as a sanctuary to nourish and revitalize yourself. Seek to create tranquility and joy in your home.

— Get regular sleep.

— Choose from the list below to find ways to nourish yourself:

— Start the day with 20-30 minutes doing something you enjoy.

— When you have lunch, take time to rest and re-create.

— Either when you return to your home from being out all day, or around dinner time, do something relaxing to release stress from the day.

— Build exercise into your daily life (example: walk everyday).

— Eat foods that are nutritious and improve your energy and mood (example: dark leafygreens; almonds, pecans, peanuts and other nuts; and orange juice).

— Avoid negativity, including things that disturb you on television, radio, newspaper and the internet. Consider going without television and other media that may bother you.

— Laugh every day

— Have quiet time to seek inner peace

— Have something to look forward to every weekend

— Do something special at least once a month

— Celebrate life whenever possible (examples: birthdays, holidays, anniversaries)

— If you do mental work, have physical exercise as a hobby

— If you do physical work, have mental exercise as a hobby

— Take time off from focusing on stressful events in your life and the outside world.

Your family, friends, neighbors, coworkers, and others in your life have emotional needs as well. Pay attention to their moods and lives. Give them a kind word, an attentive ear, a compassionate heart. They will appreciate you for it and you will learn about life from them.

There are also things to try to focus your attention on. This may help give you strength and insight about the good things in the world.

Focus on natural beauty

— Take walks in natural areas

— Have pictures of rainbows, lakes, and waterfalls to decorate your home

Focus on positive events and people.

— Remember people and things that inspire you and make you believe in goodness

— Act with gentleness, caring, and patience toward others

— See the good intentions in people around you

Have a positive spirituality.

— Pray, meditate, and otherwise do activities that make you feel closer to the Deity

— Take one day at a time

— Have patience with the unfolding of events

— Seek to trust and have faith in the universe and the Deity

Act with gentleness toward yourself and others

— Seek to not harm yourself or others

— Never trust a message saying you must do harm to yourself or others

— Remember and acknowledge those who love you, even if they don't understand you

— Be thankful and grateful for all the good things you have in your life right now

Finally, check your reality to see if others are experiencing what you are:

— Ask people if they see and hear the things you see and hear

— Check with people you trust about your ideas and experiences

— Ask people what they want for you and try to communicate why you believe what you believe

— Ask people to be patient with you as you try to explain your ideas

— Try to communicate your big ideas in ways that other people can understand—remember,they haven't experienced what you have

— Keep in mind that many coincidences and events may be metaphors and symbols, and therefore aren't literal truths

— Remember that truth is often personal, so your lessons and insights may not apply to everyone, everywhere. Your insights from the metaphors in your vision quest are your own, and you can honor them without them having to apply to all people.

By doing these things, you will help in saving yourself and your world. In time, you will be able to do many things to help others, provided you treat yourself with love and kindness now.

Remember: the Deity loves you and wants you to live a long, happy life on this Earth.

ABOUT MILT GREEK

After becoming a computer programmer in 1989 following developing schizophrenia during college, Milt Greek volunteered extensively with individuals in psychosis and post-psychosis. He led a schizophrenic early recovery group and has conducted subject-participation studies and surveys on psychosis. He began presenting on schizophrenia and recovery in the late 1990s and has delivered talks to mental health professionals and at conferences, and has been published on the web by the Ohio Criminal Justice Coordinating Center of Excellence. While he remains employed as a computer programmer, he devotes extensive time to sharing insights and concrete techniques for working with people in psychosis and post-psychosis.

To learn more about Milt Greek, and order DVDs of this material, visit **www.schizophreniablueprint.com**.

5994666R00104

Made in the USA
San Bernardino, CA
27 November 2013